Me AND THE Middle East

Firsthand Reporting on Israel's Most Dramatic Days

Richard Oestermann

gefen
publishing house
JERUSALEM • NEW YORK Est. 1981

COVER DESIGN & TYPESETTING: Benjie Herskowitz, Etc. Studios
Photograph of author on back cover by David Rubinger

ISBN: 978-965-229-737-2

1 3 5 7 9 8 6 4 2

Gefen Publishing House Ltd.
6 Hatzvi Street
Jerusalem 94386, Israel
972-2-538-0247
orders@gefenpublishing.com

Gefen Books
11 Edison Place
Springfield, NJ 07081
516-593-1234
orders@gefenpublishing.com

www.gefenpublishing.com

Printed in Israel   *Send for our free catalog*

_____

Library of Congress Control Number: 2014948308

To Iris

Contents

Preface

I wrote this book because I felt that I had to.

I wrote it because I thought that it was about time that some of all that I have experienced through a rich life be read by as many as possible. I want these experiences – perhaps enough for more than one life – to be widely read.

For years I have been encouraged to write my memoirs but have declined, as they cannot be complete because I have promised to protect my sources.

But then also this house of cards fell. Because of illness I decided to write as fast as possible about my life for the benefit of my family. This I did in the early summer of 2013, when I privately published my small, family-directed memoir *On the Sunny Side of the Street* – because that is how I experienced the first part of my lifetime: sunlit. In my illness I remembered a line by the great Danish psalm/songwriter B. S. Ingemann (1841) that reads "Nobody knows the day until the sun sets" (in Danish: "Ingen kender dagen før solen går ned").

After I published my small, personal book, I felt pressure from outsiders. "It's here and now," they said, "that you must write extensively about your time in the Middle East, including your escapades in the Arab world, which you have never done before."

So this I did, and in the process discovered which bigwigs I have interviewed – Truman, Ben-Gurion, Begin, Kollek, Agnon, Sophia Loren. I also wrote about my experiences with Sadat and Begin and my personal experiences during Israel's wars. And then, of course, whether I see any way out of this deep conflict.

So here is the memoir about me and the Middle East. For its creation I am exceedingly grateful to my partner, art historian Iris Fishof, for her untiring support, and to the young Danish social volunteer, Maria Hoffmann, because she was eager for the book and with her eminent knowledge of English and computers she participated in its coming into being.

Half a hundred stories, big and small, and almost as many illustrations. Some of these stories are veritable scoops.

And which story do I like best myself? Perhaps my interview with Harry S Truman, but several others are standing in line.

Richard Oestermann,
Summer 2014

Sources

How did I correctly establish what went on many years ago, in minute details?

Here is the revelation.

Throughout my long life as a journalist I have taken the time to put my articles in scrapbooks – just to keep them. I never thought of them as source material. Whenever I received my stories printed up in Danish, Norwegian, Swedish and Finnish newspapers, I placed them in scrapbooks. I have more than fifty such volumes.

The author with one of his scrapbooks (Photo by Debbi Cooper)

I do not know of any other journalist who keeps what he/she has written in such a way. I have willed all my scrapbooks to the Royal Library in Copenhagen for use by students of the Middle East, and the chief librarian has confirmed that the Royal Library will pay for the cost of shipment. It will be a major expense, but they have assured me in writing that they will undertake this.

Only when I decided last summer that now is the time to write about my life as journalist, did I realize that I had all the source material next to me. I could just consult with the albums to check what the major stories were in a particular year – and then I could actually quote myself.

Now I have revealed my work secret.

It was a lot of heavy work taking the scrapbooks, each weighing some ten pounds, down from the shelves to examine them. But then I realized that I had an actual goldmine at hand.

A publisher said to me: "You must tell your readers about your scrapbooks. Today everything is on computer. No journalist would ever think of doing what you have done. Your work method will give even more authenticity to your book."

Fascination

The Middle East has fascinated me for as long as I can remember – all the way back to the time when the area was called the Near East, during World War II. It probably started to interest me during the war, when focus was on the Allied victories in this part of the world, and when Israel came into existence in 1948.

This book will have a personal touch and will be written in first person (difficult for a journalist), as it deals with my work as a Middle East correspondent over more than fifty years and my escapades in the Arab world.

The book is a kind of memoir – "kind of" because I believe I may know too much, and I promised my sources never to reveal what they told me. I am sticking to my promise. I will take these secrets with me to somewhere. Some of the people who gave me this information are no longer alive. How could I betray them?

So, rather let sleeping dogs lie.

I have often asked myself whether a journalist belonging to the Jewish faith can cover the Middle East adequately, without taking the side of the strongman here, Israel. My answer is – yes, he can, if only he has the rights of the Palestinians in mind and writes in an evenhanded, balanced way. That I have tried to do for more than five decades.

There is also an advantage to being a Jewish journalist covering the Middle East. Such a person has a much deeper insight into Jewish matters than any outsider and is able to contribute his knowledge of various situations. Admitted, an entirely neutral attitude to the Arab-Jewish situation hardly exits, but precisely because of such presumed bias, a Jewish correspondent here may cover the region in a more comprehensive way than others.

To cover the Middle East story – whether your base is Amman, Jerusalem or elsewhere – you must have an indomitable curiosity, be mentally and physically strong, and never take no for an answer. Wherever you are in whichever circumstances, you must remember to be the "effendi," the authoritative person, who is not to be pushed over. I have exercised this attitude wherever I have been in my exploits in the Arab world – in Jordan, Egypt and Lebanon.

The Middle East entered my consciousness already in my boyish years in Copenhagen, where the Jewish community, to which I belonged, was appalled over the Arab killings of sixty-seven Jews in Hebron in 1929. As a twelve-year-old I had a kind of blood connection with the then Palestine, as my half-brother, Irmond Leon Oestermann, was killed by Arabs in an ambush on the serpentine road, winding up from Haifa down below to Kibbutz Bet Oren on the Carmel Mountain.

Credo

I have a credo. I believe that the area in which we live must be divided between Jews and Arabs as a necessity for peace – that Israel cannot go on ruling a large, hostile Arab minority, if it wants to remain a democratic, Jewish state.

Over the course of my career I have tried to cover the rise of the Sunnis and Shiites, each funded by oil money, trying to purge the other in various Middle East countries. I believe that it all boils down to economics. That the Arabs may recognize that the existence of Israel is to their good. They can learn from Israel how to increase their standard of living – that the little man who has a small car is an example to follow for a person only possessing a donkey.

I have also learned that it takes Muslim moderates to abolish Muslim extremists.

As *New York Times* columnist Thomas L. Friedman recently wrote: "Hizbollah started a war against Israel in 2008, without knowing how to end it. It didn't matter whether it won or lost. All that mattered was that it 'resisted the Zionists.'"

The decisive epoch in my journalistic life was when I attended the Adolf Eichmann trial in Jerusalem in early 1961.

But before I reach so far – here is my earlier life.

1926–1957:

Growing Up in Denmark

Family Background

My entry into this world was on May 19, 1926, at 35 Vesterbrogade, in downtown Copenhagen. I was born at home, like two of my three older sisters. My oldest sister, Else, was born at the Ladies Esman's Children's Clinic. Else, Margot and Lillian are no longer alive. I feel such a longing for them. I have nobody to share childhood experiences with but myself. I can never check the correctness of my childhood thoughts. But, of course, I share this predicament with many.

I was closest to my sister Margot, three years older than me, possibly because of her attitude to the theater world. She became an actress and I also wanted to join the theater, but was flunked.

Left to right: Margot, Lilian, my mother, myself, my father and Else, Humlebæk, 1930

My father, Moritz (Meir) Oestermann, came to Denmark by accident. He was the son of Samuel Oestermann, a merchant, and his wife Fanny (née Slavitzki). He was born in Charol, near Poltava in the Ukraine. I always remember my father describing the road from Charol to Poltava, full of cherry trees in blossom, with a great scent, as he put it. I also remember that he was a soldier, which was rare for Jews in Russia. He served in the Caucasus, and never stopped telling his children about nature there, with all the eagles.

Following a pogrom in 1905, my father wanted to immigrate to the United States. En route was Copenhagen, and – as my father told us many times over the years – there my father said, "This looks good enough for me." And then he descended, holding a samovar in one hand and a hanukkiah in the other. I later saw an exact copy of the bronze candelabra in a restaurant in Tel Aviv, where they told me that they only knew it came from Russia. His landing in Denmark was my luck; otherwise I could not have told the following. I still have his candelabra.

My father had little education, but, I learned much later, got a job at a Copenhagen weapons factory, Riffelsyndikatet. I have no idea what this job entailed. Perhaps it was related to his knowledge of weapons as a Russian soldier? Later he became a manufacturer of men's hats, with his own shop. It was located at 28 Amagerbrogade on the island of Amager, just south of Copenhagen proper. Now and then he would do very well and come home with lots of money, at other times there was nothing. Pentecost was his great season, as Danish men wanted to sport new and elegant headgear at springtime.

I came into the world on the first day of the Jewish holiday of Shavuot. The day I was born, my father came into the synagogue beaming. "What happened to you, Moritz?" the worshippers asked. "You look so happy! Did you get a new walking stick?" "No," my father replied, "I got a son."

The Lure Blowers

My father married Paula Henriette Vilhelmine (née Wagner) of Hamburg before World War I. She was the sister of sculptor Siegfried Wagner (born 1874), famous for his statue of Viking lure blowers (in Danish: "Lurblæserne") which was placed in Copenhagen's town hall square in 1914, one hundred years ago. He died in Lyngby, near Copenhagen, in 1914.

Paula also died in Copenhagen in 1914, when she was only thirty-six years old. She and my father had three children: Eleanor (born in Copenhagen in 1907), Asta (born 1909) and Irmond Leon (born 1910).

When my father married my mother Gertrud (née Grün), these children lived elsewhere in Copenhagen. All three had a cosmopolitan outlook. Eleanor lived during World War II in Casablanca (75 Rue d'Anfa, I still remember). After the war she sent us packages from Morocco with clothes and goodies. Later she married Willy Kastendeich. They had a road inn in France, near the border with Germany, and I visited them there some fifty years ago. Eleanor has a daughter, Bente, married, who lives in Hillerød. Bente visited us in Copenhagen, but we do not have any contact now. Asta joined the Allied Forces during World War II and was employed by UNRWA, traveling on help missions through postwar Europe.

Throughout my childhood it was rumored that we were descendants of a Russian noble family by the same family name, although without the *e*. One of the ancestors was supposedly Heinrich (Andrej Ivanovitch) Ostermann, a count who served the Russian czar as a statesman. The idea of hailing from this man, I later checked, is nonsensical, but there is a marble statue of his wife, Countess Ostermann, at the entrance to the Thorvaldsen Museum in Copenhagen.

Teaching Immigrants

My mother never had a formal education but she spoke a beautiful Danish, very rich. One day the chief rabbi, Professor David Simonsen, asked her whether she would teach the Danish language to newly arrived immigrants from Germany and other parts of Europe. She accepted – provided she could teach them something about Danish culture as well. She had many students. One of them was a Dr. Rafael Edelmann, who later became a chief librarian at the Copenhagen Royal Library. In this capacity he was in charge of its vast Jewish literary treasure, with many thousands of books donated by Professor Simonsen from his private collection.

My mother asked Edelmann whether he would teach me Judaism, because I went to a non-Jewish school and was lacking in my Jewish knowledge. Rafael Edelmann agreed. And so it came to pass that the Edelmanns and the Oestermanns got into a pendulum show of gratitude. Years later, Edelmann's son Martin (Moshe) asked me whether I would review the text to his doctoral thesis, "The Oath in the Bible," for the University of Copenhagen, because his Danish after many years abroad had become somewhat rusty. The Copenhagen university made it a condition that I should correct his manuscript. I agreed, in gratitude of his father's tutelage.

After helping Martin with his thesis for the whole of the following year, the next step in this saga was when my two sons, both competitive swimmers, taught Martin's children to swim. Then there was a follow-up – Martin prepared both my sons for bar mitzvah and years later officiated at their weddings.

My mother descended directly from a certain Moshe Salomonsen, also called Mausche Nyborg, whose family had come to Germany from Poland in the seventeenth century and later settled in the Danish town Nyborg. He was born there in 1695 and became a tobacco merchant. King Christian IV (1588–1648) had invited Jews from central Europe to Denmark to help improve its economy, which had suffered from fatiguing wars with Sweden. My mother's father, Herman, and grandfather Salomon were born in Copenhagen. Thus Jews have lived in Denmark for some four hundred years – and I am a kind of "Mayflower" Danish Jew on my mother's side.

My grandfather, Herman Grün, standing next to a large Mercedes Benz car owned by his two well-to-do sons Hugo and Laurits. They were about to take him to a weekly meeting of learned Danish Jews, where he presided over talks on religious matters. The picture was taken on March 31, 1931, when he was eighty-five years old.

My mother Gertrud was one of ten children – six boys and four girls. Somehow it fell to her to become the great mediator, solving problems and intrigues that were unavoidable in such a diverse family. Addi and Erna, the wives of the two rich sons, Hugo and Laurits, were jealous of one another in various materialistic matters, such as having chauffeur-driven cars and fur coats.

It turned into a family feud, to the point that we no longer had big family get-togethers. Then one day it happened that Addi and Erna appeared, holding hands. "This is Gertrud's work," was the comment. True enough, Gertrud had taken the two ladies aside and talked words of wisdom with each of them and eventually they saw the pettiness of their arguments and made peace.

Irmond

The twenty-year-old adventurer, before he went to Palestine

Irmond, my father's son from his first marriage with Paula, was my great hero, and I idolized him. At that time we lived in an apartment in Vesterbrogade in downtown Copenhagen.

Of my three half siblings, Irmond Leon was my man. He was sixteen years older than me, but we were great friends. I adored him. His character showed when he, coming home from a long trip in the Canadian forests, used to say, "Denmark is too small for me, I am an adventurer." He was given a florist's shop in Frederiksberg, a gift from our father. One day Irmond showed up at our summerhouse in Vedbæk, some twelve miles north of Copenhagen. He had bicycled all the way and was dripping with sweat. "I have a customer in the shop," he said, "who wanted to buy some fern. I didn't have it in the shop, but I knew we had some in the garden here."

So he rode off, with our fern. Whether his customer was still at his shop, waiting for him, I do not know.

But I do know that Irmond had a friend from Palestine, a tall man with a lot of dark hair, by the name of Joe Kagan. They visited us in Vedbæk and I remember them sprinting side by side on the quiet villa roads. They took turns winning the race – to everyone's great admiration.

And I shall never forget that Irmond bought me a one-yard-long sailing ship, which we took from our apartment in Vesterbrogade to the dragon fountain in the town hall square, and we had it sail around the dragon, round and round. Today the big water basin as it was then has shrunk into something much smaller.

Joe and Irmond left for Palestine sometime in the mid-1930s. This was the last I saw of my brother. We had a lot of correspondence with him, though. We waited anxiously for his letters because he was so young, in his early twenties, when he left Denmark for an area that we all knew was dangerous.

When Irmond first got to Palestine he worked in the Tel Aviv harbor. Later he moved to Kibbutz Bet Oren, of which he was a founding member. It is near the Carmel Forest in the Haifa area. The words "Ya'arot Carmel" (the Carmel Forest) became part of my childhood.

Their kibbutz was like what we know from westerns, with wooden sticks all around. In the evening, the kibbutz members sat around a bonfire, telling stories to keep their spirits up. One of the best storytellers was Irmond, who was admired for his tall tales from the Canadian forests. The adventurer spoke.

Little did they know that a disaster was around the corner. One day in August 1938, a team of some eight to ten people from the kibbutz went down to Haifa on a weekly trip to buy food. When they returned, coming up the narrow, curvy road, an Arab ambush was waiting for them.

The Arabs, way outnumbering the Jews, were hiding behind stone walls. The kibbutznikim had taken the stones away from the kibbutz ground in order to cultivate the area.

Irmond, only twenty-five years old, was one of the people on the truck. And so was his wife, Egyptian-born Ahuva, twenty years old and pregnant with their first child. When the ambush began, the kibbutz members on the truck turned their vehicle over and used it as a barricade. Ahuva fought alongside the men. The Jews fought until they were no more. They were all killed, except one who pretended that he was dead. Ahuva and their unborn child also died. Rumors report that there were eighty Arabs against eight kibbutz members.

It was a devastating event. I have read about it the annals of the kibbutz. In Danish newspapers, as well, it was written up on the front page
that a Dane had fallen in Palestine in a fight with Arabs.

As the news reached Copenhagen, two men rang the doorbell of our
apartment in Peder Skramsgade, near the Royal Theater on the Kongens
Nytorv Square. They wanted to talk to my father and were shown into
his study. Although I was only twelve years old, I remember the name
of one of the men – Maurice Laserson – who had come up from Paris,
together with another man, to see my father. They told him about the
ambush. Then I heard a shrill sound – my father crying out as he heard
that Irmond had been killed.

This sound still rings in my ears and may have contributed to the
fact that I myself went to Israel.

I learned more about Irmond when I came to Israel in 1952 on my
first visit, already a journalist then, writing for Scandinavian newspapers.
I asked my guide to take me to the cemetery at the southern entrance
to Haifa, with its black door adorned by a golden Magen David, established for heroes and heroines who had fallen in battle with the Arabs.
The guide found Irmond's grave, with Ahuva's close to it. I said Kaddish,
the Jewish prayer for a deceased family member. Then a man appeared,
saying: "Who are you, why do you say Kaddish here?" I explained. And
he said, "Go back to your hotel and I will send you somebody who knew
your brother." So Yitzhak Risch appeared. He had lived in the kibbutz and
known Irmond well. Yitzhak was dressed like in the old days, with short
pants and stockings to the knee.

He told me that one of the persons ambushed had pretended to be
dead. "His name is Berger, a laundry owner in Kiryat Tivon, north of
Haifa," Yitzhak said.

"Call him," Yitzhak said. "He has a lot to tell."

This was at the end of my visit to the country, and I only saw Berger
during my next visit to Israel in 1958. Berger showed me photos of Irmond
and Ahuva that I had never seen, a happy young couple. And he even
showed me some correspondence between Irmond and the Jewish community in Copenhagen. Irmond had asked the Danish Jews to contribute
to buying an armor-plated vehicle. But there had not been any response.
The Jews in Denmark had not understood what he was talking about.

Berger told me about Irmond's influence on the mood in the kibbutz, when people were fearful of Arab attacks.

"Your brother kept our morale high," Berger said. "We sat around the bonfire in the evening, hoping that the night would pass quietly, without an attack. Your brother was a good storyteller. He was an imaginative soul and he could make up stories on the spot. He used to tell us all about life in the big Canadian forests."

Later my father was informed that a piece of land in the kibbutz belonged to Irmond, but my father, now the owner of the plot, with a gentle gesture said that he would give it back to the kibbutz.

Irmond is mentioned once a year in the Copenhagen Great Synagogue, among the names of renowned Jewish men and women. Years later I managed to get a medal and a citation from the Ministry of Defense, in memory of Irmond. He and Ahuva are recognized as heroes. I have this recognition, framed, in front of my desk where I am writing now.

I have visited Kibbutz Bet Oren several times and met with older members who knew Irmond and Ahuva. They told me some things I did not know, among others about the armored vehicle.

Irmond's death was a turning point in my life.

His fate and that of Ahuva's are written up in a book published by the Israeli Defense Ministry about the disturbances – as this mini war was called – in the Haifa area.

Educated by Andersens

I got a comprehensive education at Østre Borgerdyd Gymnasium in Copenhagen, established in 1787 (before the French Revolution), and I still send glowing thoughts of appreciation to my old school for having given me an encompassing knowledge of the classics, of languages – with a stress on English – of how to use books and, above all, a good Danish. I am still grateful to my alma mater. Without this background I would never have made it into English-language journalism.

Rector Einer Andersen, 1937

We were introduced to how to use books when our rector, Einer Andersen, teacher of German and ancient Nordic languages, one day said: "Boys, everything is in the books, you only have to learn how to use them." And so he taught us how to use dictionaries, encyclopedias, reference books and thesauri. He named the course "Use of Books," to be taught once a week. We always looked forward to those eye-opening lessons. Still today, I hardly write any article without having a number of such books around me, to be used according to the Andersen principle.

Rector Andersen and I became friends. He let me use his big library during breaks, as much as I desired. The history of World War I was my great interest, and he had a lot of books on that subject. There I came across James Joyce's *Ulysses* and later bragged that I had read it. Nonsense – it was way above me. But I wanted to show off.

Andersen was pointed out by a Danish Nazi paper as being Jew friendly. We were several Jewish boys in the school and never felt like outsiders. One of my classmates, Jørgen E. Nielsen, now a retired physician, told me that one day at the end of October, following the Nazi persecution of the Danish Jews, Andersen came into our classroom and said, tears running down his cheeks: "Boys, I am so happy. I just learned today that the last of my Jewish boys arrived safely in Sweden."

We were taught English by Danish teachers who had studied in England. One English teacher by the name of Heskjær (I do not remember his first name and cannot find it after seventy years) greatly amused us. He did not mind making himself ridiculous in the eyes of his pupils as long as he could get his message across.

"The difficult word *immediately*," he would say. "I will teach you to spell correctly so you will never forget how to do it." And with that Heskjær moved in front of the lectern and started jumping up and down, fingers accompanying him, shouting "im," "me," "di" "a," "te," "ly," while we screamed with laughter – but never forgot the spelling.

We began learning English when we were only eleven years old. I was deeply impressed when some of my classmates – ordinary Danish boys – began speaking English to each other. "We just want to practice what we have learned," they said.

At that time I had coined the following phrase: "I love life, I just could not live without it." It may sound corny. So what? It has resonated with me all my life.

I believe I have lived much of my adult life with Hans Christian Andersen in one hand and William Shakespeare in the other. Both writers helped form my life, I dare to say. At school I tried hard to get behind the Shakespearean words to understand what Shakespeare had intended. And, much later, I visited the theater by the Thames in London. It produced Shakespearean plays performed by groups from abroad, in their languages.

And Andersen. I knew many of his thrilling fairy tales, but one especially, "The Shirt Collar" (in Danish: "Flipperne"). When I was twenty and tried to become an actor, I knew how to enact this fairy tale almost as a professional actor. And then there was – above them all, I believe – "The Ugly Duckling" ("Den grimme ælling"), who started out as a miserable black duckling, and turned into a white, majestic swan. Whenever I was in trouble, I thought of the philosophy and wisdom of Andersen's words, changed by me into: "First you go through something awful – and then you become famous."

As I have mentioned, another genius Andersen was the rector of my school, Einer Andersen, who was a major force in giving his some three hundred boy pupils a wide-ranging education. Fifty years later my former classmates and I established a scholarship foundation in the name of this stalwart, humanitarian educator, to be used by not-as-well-heeled high school students so they could go on school trips in Europe (Paris, London, etc.) with their more well-to-do classmates. Among the contributors was the Danish-American entertainer, Victor Borge, who attended my school long before me.

For me, Einer Andersen's greatness is encapsulated in a meeting I had with him in June 1945. At that time I was a refugee in Sweden. I was studying at a high school in Lund while simultaneously training as a soldier in the Danish brigade, a fighting force established in Sweden to help drive the Germans out of Denmark. In uniform, I visited Andersen at his school. He then said: "I would like you to come next week for graduation day, so you can stand with all your classmates to get a rector handshake, because I want you to know that you are not only a graduate from the Danish high school in Lund, but from our school as well."

Wartime

My school achieved the reputation that it had more saboteurs against the Germans than any other school in Denmark. High school boys, just sixteen and seventeen years old, went out at night to commit acts of sabotage against the Germans, and innocently showed up in class the next day. I wanted to join them but was told that it would be unwise for a Jewish boy to do so, as it might hasten persecution of Jews in Denmark. But I was allowed to become a distributor of underground newspapers – also a very dangerous job. It involved going to a post office and mailing envelopes containing the paper, but without a return address, to special people, and distributing it in the school, but only to certain pupils.

At that time the Germans were against any Western influence, including jazz. But my friends and I loved jazz, and Copenhagen had many jazz restaurants, among them Blue Heaven in Vesterport, where the great jazz violinist Svend Asmussen and his band played.

Back then it was forbidden for young people under the age of sixteen to go to restaurants in the evening without carrying the written consent of their parents. When the waiter came to the table where I sat with some friends, he asked to see their parental letters. "It's OK, waiter," I said. "They're together with me." I was only fifteen years old then, but looked older.

My best friend then was Niels Ebbe Bindslev, called "Nebber," whose father was a member of parliament and one of the mayors of Copenhagen. Nebber and I went to numerous parties together. When the Germans imposed curfew from early evening and throughout the night, we managed to dodge this – we had night parties, arriving in pajamas and sporting a toothbrush in the buttonhole.

I escaped from Denmark in a dramatic way. On September 26, 1943 – I remember the date because it was the birthday of King Christian X – a friend of mine, jazz-drummer Pedro Bieker, warned me of the imminent persecution of Jews and admonished me and my family to take shelter.

King Christian X was in the hearts of all Danes, because of his valiant and brave opposition to the occupation. There are many myths about him and the German occupiers. Few of these stories are true. For example, the king never wore an armband with the word "Jude." The Jews in Denmark were never exposed to this.

But the following anecdote may very well be true. On the day of occupation, April 9, 1940, the German commander, General von Kaupisch, ran the swastika up the mast of swanky Hotel d'Angleterre, headquarters of the German army. The king called the general and told him to take the flag down.

"It will not happen," Kaupisch said. "Then I will send a Danish soldier to take it down," the king said. "The soldier will be shot," said Kaupisch. "I am the Danish soldier," Christian said. The flag was taken down, though soon after it was hoisted again.

Whenever I tell this story, I feel it down my spine. Also now.

Fleeing to Sweden

My family was made up of my mother, Gertrud (aged sixty), and my two older sisters, Margot (twenty) and Lillian (eighteen). During the last days of September 1943 we stayed with friends and acquaintances in Humlebæk and Snekkersten – small fishing villages and summer resort sites – and with the help of a young resistance man, Eyvind Skjær, a close friend of Margot's and myself, we found a chance to go by fishing boat to Sweden on October 1, in the late evening – the time set by the Germans to start the action against the Jews.

Originally, we were supposed to use an escape route from Gilleleje, a fishing village and resort place some twelve miles west of Elsinore. We were lucky that this plan was canceled. Had we gone by way of Gilleleje we would most certainly have been sent to the Theresienstadt concentration camp, as were all Jewish refugees hiding there, who were informed on by a Danish Nazi and deported. Fortunately, Eyvind found another route and made an agreement with fisherman Andersen from the nearby fishing village of Espergærde to pick us up. We looked forward to meeting the man who was to be our savior.

The transport cost 1,000 kr. per person, a huge amount then, but not so big when one considered that one's life was at stake. My mother did not have 4,000 kr., but received it from a wealthy brother with the words: "My treasure box is open to the whole family." As my mother was one of ten siblings, this was quite a generous offer. People who could not raise this amount got to Sweden free of charge. The Danish resistance movement took care of that.

Our flight was a dangerous undertaking. We were to be picked up at midnight by fisherman Andersen. Eyvind got us together and we moved in darkness through the Lave Skov Forest, toward the Nivå Bay. It was a chilly evening, with a few clouds in the dark sky. When we got out of the forest, we were on the coastal road Copenhagen-Elsinore. We saw Gestapo cars, with lights on, going up and down the road, looking for Jews.

When we saw no lights, we crossed the road, hurriedly. We came to a kind of pier that shot out into a bay. We walked fast, led by Eyvind. At the end of the pier was a door, with a big padlock. Eyvind and I looked at one another – and opened the lock, with unimaginable force. We will never know whether it was rusty or perhaps not locked. But we opened it.

On the other side of the door, on a concrete platform, we were to meet Andersen. On land we could hear the screams of Jews who were caught by the Germans. This was the place where my two cousins, Olaf and Johan, were taken by the Nazis the day after we escaped, and deported to Theresienstadt. They returned to Denmark in May 1945, in bad shape.

It was difficult to play this waiting game. We stood on the platform, fearing for our lives. Nothing happened. The time went on. We shivered in the dark. Then we heard the motor of a boat approaching – Andersen was coming. He got us onboard. He ordered me to stay on deck and pretend that I was his fisher boy.

A German patrol boat came by. There were three men on board. Our luck – had there been more than that they might have informed on one another. But presumably all three knew one another and they kept their secret. The patrol boat turned around. The Germans muttered something to the effect of "Let the devils go."

En route fisherman Andersen and I pulled a trick on the Germans. I was in a blue fisherman's sweater Andersen had given me, and he and I pretended that we were pulling fishing nets aboard and shouted to one another about the good haul.

There are three outstanding Andersens in my life – my rector Einer Andersen, the fairy tale writer Hans Christian Andersen and, of course, the fisherman who saved us.

With the Germans behind us, we charted our course toward Sweden. We could see lights on the Swedish coast. In Denmark all was utter darkness. About a hundred yards from land, Andersen determined by means of an oar that the water was only three feet deep. He told us that this would be where we had to get off. He did not dare go closer to the border, fearing that his boat might be confiscated by the Swedes for his "illegal" activity – and, after all, he had to go back to pick up more refugees.

I was the first to go overboard. The water went all the way up to my neck. I had placed my shoes in my coat pocket, but they quickly floated away. Then my two sisters got into the water. They were both competitive swimmers and helped our mother, who could not swim.

Suddenly, I noticed that Margot's raincoat was about to become entangled in the propeller of the boat. I shouted up to Andersen from the dark, murky waters: "Stop the engine!" He heard me and I freed the coat. The episode ended well, but it has been a gruesome theme in my nightmares for years. We continued, half swimming, half wading.

It was dawn as we came up on the Swedish island of Hven, with its steep slopes. Now I could really appreciate what it meant to have lost my shoes. My bare feet were bleeding from walking on sharp rocks and pieces of broken glass.

But we were safe.

Two Swedish soldiers stood on a cliff and regarded this wet and forlorn little group. "Welcome to old Sweden," they shouted. And then they cried. So did we, our tears mingling with the waters of the Øresund.

In the early morning hours, the soldiers escorted us across the island to an inn, where we were given lodging. There we met many of Copenhagen's Jewish aristocracy, who we had seen a few days before in their home city, in all their elegance and self-confidence. Overnight we had all become refugees, without any earthly possessions. Some, like myself, were wearing three shirts, one on top of the other. Nobody had any luggage.

The following day we continued on via Hven to Landskrona on the Swedish mainland. In Sweden our little family began life as refugees, a situation that lasted a year and a half. We remained there until May 1945. But that is another story.

Our luck, combined with the determined efforts of the Danish people and the resistance movement on behalf of the Danish Jews, became our salvation. It could just as well have gone wrong, as it did for my two cousins, Olaf and Johan.

Invented

I once said in an interview with a Danish newspaper that if Denmark did not exist, it had to be invented. Its people are special and care about others. It is not only that the Danes rescued 90 percent of the Danish-Jewish population, and welcomed them home after the war. More than anything else they became a glowing example of how humanity should be.

I firmly believe that the rescue in Denmark helped Europe regain some measure of decency and morality.

The question has been raised many times: Why was it only the Danes who made such a humanitarian effort to save Jews from the Nazis' claws? Danish clergyman Ivor Lange, of the Frederiksberg Church in Copenhagen, gave this answer: "Those who remain silent and only show their aversion by shrugging their shoulders are no better than the Nazi collaborators. I would rather die with the Jews than live with the Nazis."

There is something very humane in Denmark that is likened to the biblical notion of "I am my brother's keeper." A massive rejection of the Germans because of their attitude toward the Jews became prevalent in the Danish population. Many Danes felt deeply angry with what was happening to their Jewish fellow citizens. And the feeling gained legitimacy when, at the end of September 1943, all the bishops in Denmark wrote a protest to the German authorities, a document that was read from every pulpit.

Among other things it said: "The persecution of the Jews is contrary to human comprehension and compassion, which is the message that Christ's church is set to proclaim. Such persecution is contrary to the sense of justice that is prevalent among the Danish people, ingrained in our Danish Christian culture throughout centuries. We will fight so that our Jewish brothers and sisters will keep the same freedom as we ourselves value more than life itself."

What is the Danes' perception of their Jewish fellow citizens today? This question was put by me to Pastor Esper Thiedemann from Aarhus, who, some years ago, filled in as the Danish priest in Jerusalem. He said to me in an interview in July 1998: "If an equivalent situation should arise for Danish Jews today, I am convinced that the Danes would react the same way. I am proud that the majority of Danish Jews were rescued."

The current Danish attitude toward the Jews is reflected in a book written by the Danish newspaper *Politiken*'s chief editor, Bo Lidegård, who gave his encompassing book about the rescue operation, published in 2013, the expressive title *Compatriots* ("Landsmænd").

Swedish Haven

The Danish-Jewish exodus to Sweden lasted three weeks. It set out from remote places in Denmark, wherever it was feasible. About 7,000 Danish Jews escaped, while 481 were captured and deported to Theresienstadt. The majority of these came back to Denmark after the liberation in May 1945.

In addition to giving refuge to the Danish Jews, Sweden also became a haven for some four thousand other Danes, among them people from the resistance movement and central European Jews who had found refuge in Denmark, as well as Communists and Allied airmen who had been shot down over Danish territory.

In Sweden I enlisted as a student at the Danish high school established in the university town of Lund. The school's academic level was high. Some of our teachers were celebrities. Our teacher of mathematics was none other than Professor Harald Bohr, brother of the Nobel prize winner in physics Niels Bohr.

I shall not dwell on details of the following one and a half years as a seventeen-year-old youngster, all by myself without any family close by. The rest of the family was in faraway Stockholm. I will only say that it was a maturing experience.

Many young Danish refugees in Sweden, Jews or non-Jews, enlisted in the secret Danish army that was being formed in Sweden, with the goal of joining the Allied forces in the liberation of Denmark. It comprised saboteurs, other members of the resistance movement and Danish Jews. This military unit, totaling five thousand men and women, was called the Danforce Brigade, and I was one of the first to join up with them.

Our unit in the Danish brigade, some of us trained in Sweden by British commando soldiers, helped slightly in freeing Denmark from the occupation. We wanted so much to use our weapons against them, but there were very few incidents.

Gun affairs were among the highlights of my time in Sweden. I was involved in most of them. At an early stage I acquired a revolver – I will never tell how – to be sent on to the resistance movement in Denmark and used against the Germans. I hid it in a suitcase so that my roommate, a young saboteur by the name of Torsten, should never see it – but he did. And gone was the gun.

I moved to another place in Lund and bought a new revolver from a Swedish acquaintance. It was also put away in a suitcase, but one day my new roommate, Bent, a young saboteur from Elsinore, saw me cleaning the gun. I told him never to touch it.

But coming home from school one day, I saw water gushing down the staircase and ran up. There was Bent, his face pale, holding a smoking gun. He had accidentally shot a hole in a central heating radiator, from which water was now streaming out. He could just as well have hit two young Swedish girls, who were sitting on a sofa in an adjoining room. I took the gun from Bent, well knowing that the Swedish police were on their way. Quickly we invented the story that we had had a mock fight with pointed sticks and that one of them had penetrated the radiator. We knew that nobody would believe such a story, but we decided to stick to it.

I ran away with the gun in my pocket and buried it in a park, certain that nobody was watching me. But the next day this gun was also gone – somebody must have seen me.

There was also a third weapons affair, but I was not directly involved in it. We refugee children, aged seven to eighteen, went to school in a former Swedish teachers' college, where several rooms belonged to the Swedish home guard and had stocks of weapons. A few of my saboteur classmates wanted to steal some of the weapons in order to smuggle them to the resistance movement in Denmark.

One day they decided to take a number of guns, and the next day Swedish police came to our classroom and said "this one," "this one" and "that one," pointing out suspicious-looking pupils and arresting them. It did not become a major case. The three boys were thrown out of school in a rather mild way – and transferred to another Danish high school, in Gothenburg.

Denmark Is Liberated

We closely followed the Allies' and the Red Army's progress in conquering the Germans. The Norwegian refugees in Sweden also had a secret military unit, prepared for the liberation of Norway. We Danish soldiers thought that we would join the Norwegians in liberating Norway, and we learned winter warfare from our officers. But it did not happen. Denmark was liberated before Norway.

On May 4, ears stuck to the radio, we heard that the Germans in Denmark, northwest Germany and Holland had surrendered. We reported to our military base and that same night we drove in military trucks with no lights on to the harbor in Malmö, from where our unit was to continue to Denmark.

We loaded a major part of what was to go to the resistance movement in Denmark – boots, uniforms, explosives and – so the rumor went – airplanes packed down. We had enormous strength that night, because what we did mattered. We moved heavy crates as if they were matchboxes.

The depot ship onto which we loaded material for the resistance had the name of *Røsnæs*. A six-thousand-ton freighter, it would come to play a role in Danish history.

There were some two hundred thousand German soldiers in Norway, whom the Germans wanted to move to other fronts. They first planned to bring the soldiers back to Germany, but incessant sabotage attacks against the north-south railroad line in Jutland made that impossible. The next plan was to send them by ship to France, to help boost the sagging western front. To prevent this, the resistance movement conducted several sabotage attacks against the Langebro bridge, which connects Copenhagen proper with the island of Amager.

When Langebro was repaired once more, a new phase in the resistance movement's long-term plan of preventing the German soldiers from moving south began. This was strategy at a high level. The ship *Røsnæs*, one of the vessels stuck in Copenhagen's inner port, was moved by tugboats and passed the heavily guarded Langebro into Øresund, the strait separating Denmark from Sweden. At this stage a large number of resistance men swarmed up from the hold of the ship and took over the command of it. They ran it aground on the Swedish island of Hven and called for the assistance of Danish tugboats to free it.

When the first of these tugboats, whose task is to navigate big ships through a harbor, arrived, resistance men boarded the ship and ordered it to Sweden. This act repeated itself until there were no more tugboats left in Danish waters. They were all in Swedish ports. And the German soldiers in Norway could no longer get to the western front by sea.

This strategic plan contributed to the fact that the Danish resistance movement was named "second to none" in Europe by Field Marshal Bernard Montgomery, and that Denmark was placed definitively among the Allies.

The author as a nineteen-year old soldier in the Danforce Brigade, shortly after Denmark was liberated on May 4, 1945. Background: Copenhagen's town hall square.

An Episode in Elsinore

We young soldiers spent the first hours after the liberation on *Røsnæs*, sailing from Malmö to Elsinore. Arriving in Elsinore harbor, we discovered that a great many of its inhabitants had turned up on the shore to welcome us back home.

Røsnæs dropped anchor next to the ferryboat *Storebælt*. The next second, a major scuffle began. We knew that the main force of the Danish brigade had been moved to Copenhagen to participate in a parade, but the brigade leadership had not even retained enough soldiers in Elsinore to safeguard the arrival of *Røsnæs*. This was a setback.

Suddenly a big black car with Danish Nazis equipped with machine guns arrived on the harbor. The Nazis started firing in all directions, including at us. On the green area of Kronborg Castle, a mile away from the harbor, there were still German soldiers who would not surrender to the resistance movement, but awaited the arrival of the Allied forces.

These German soldiers got entangled in the melee of general shooting. As the fighting was about to spread to *Røsnæs*, an order came from the top commander, Admiral Frits Kjølsen, to get the ship out of Elsinore harbor because we had enough explosives onboard to kill half of the city's inhabitants. We teenage soldiers did not get into combat, although we were most eager to get the Germans out. After a few hours the harbor was almost empty of ships. We were ordered to sail to the harbor of the Tuborg breweries, in northern Copenhagen, to establish the depot for the brigade.

Resuming Life

The liberation summer of 1945 was quite wild. A new time had come. The Germans were out of the country. Life could restart. I remember clearly that I saw a sign in a shop window with the text: "Closed because of happiness." The tears ran freely.

And then there was the brutalization. What would a young Danish girl wish for a birthday present? A gun.

When I reached Copenhagen as a soldier, one of my first thoughts was: "What is the situation on Sølvtorvet?" We had our apartment there and knew the Germans' Danish henchmen had taken hold of it. With my rifle in hand I prepared to return to our home. One of my soldier friends offered to go with me, but I turned his offer down. It was my task, and nobody else's.

I had a key to the apartment and let myself in, keeping a finger on the trigger in case something should happen. I jumped from door to door as I had seen it done in western movies. There was nobody in the apartment, but it had been vandalized. Somebody had made slashes in our paintings, and the furniture upholstery had been damaged by those hooligans.

One of my first thoughts was to check on a bagful of illegal papers that I had not managed to get rid of before we fled. I found my bag with the papers intact, behind some clothes in a closet in my room. I had been worrying about their fate throughout my one and a half years in Sweden.

With the war behind me, I speculated as to what field of education I should pursue – acting or journalism? First I thought of following in my sister

Copenhagen, ca. 1947

Margot's footsteps and becoming an actor because I loved the world of the theater. She had begun her career at Frederiksberg Theater in Copenhagen and then at Aarhus Theater. When I had graduated from high school and finished my military service, I started studying to become an actor, working with one of the leading directors at the Royal Theater. Konstantin Stanislavski's book *An Actor's Work with Himself* was my bible.

But my dream fell like a house of cards. My teacher was great at both acting and teaching. Almost all of his students were accepted to the theater. I was very fond of this craft and quite good at it. I discussed various roles with my teacher. Then one day I said to him, "But I don't really know whether I will be the best."

"Out!" said my teacher. "If you start doubting yourself, I will not continue with you." That was the end of my theater career. It was the winter of 1945. I wondered what I was going to be.

I decided to study law, which would likely be useful if I became a journalist. Several classmates of mine who had wanted to become journalists already worked at newspapers. And so I decided to go in that direction.

I never regretted it. Almost seventy years later I am still busy writing.

Along the way I invented my eleventh commandment: you must never fall.

Holbæk

My first job as a journalist was on the agrarian paper *Holbæk Amtsti- dende* in Holbæk, western Zealand. I was twenty-one, the youngest person on the editorial staff. Ahead of me was an apprenticeship of several years. I did not write a good newspaper Danish, but a stilted legal Danish. I had already been warned that I may not fit in with the paper when the city editor, Christian Fogtman, said that he would give me another chance.

Fogtman told me to take editorials written by our chief editor, Hans Brix, home with me and study them for language, content and clarity. Hans Brix wrote in an analytic and elegant way, with meaning behind each word, and I sat for hours and scrutinized his texts at home in my little room. I reached my goal when Fogtman said, "It's OK, you've got it. You can stay with us."

During my two years at this paper I stumbled over some writings – poems and journal entries – composed by a much-beloved Danish author by the name of Nis Petersen, who had been a journalist apprentice at another Holbæk newspaper thirty years before me.

His papers were shown to me by a man named Poul, who had found them in a chest of drawers. I immediately realized that this was a literary goldmine. Poul let me have all the material. I visited the places that Nis P. (as he was called) had frequented many years ago – restaurants, cafés, barber's shops – and inquired about him.

I decided to write an article for the magazine of the Copenhagen paper *Politiken*. It was published on February 9, 1947, with a drawing by Carl Jensen. My article contained unknown writings by Nis P., among them poems which I interspersed throughout my article.

My story caught people's attention. I had revealed something. I wrote about Nis P.'s life in Holbæk. He lived his life simply, far from the bourgeois style, and ended up finding a balance in life. One did not know much about him, and what one knew was not enough to understand him.

My article about Nis P. in Politiken's Magazinet, *1947*

Nis P. grew up in Herning, Jutland. He worked as a journalist there before coming to Holbæk in 1917, at the age of twenty-one. He wandered through Europe with Russian beggar monks from Carelia and was deep down in Bulgaria with a gipsy tribe, where he was admitted as a tribe member. He lived a freebooter existence.

Carnegie

After living in Holbæk some months I suddenly became well-known overnight. It was a warm spring day and people rushed to the Holbæk Fjord baths for a swim. We journalist apprentices were, as usual, together. Then we heard someone shout out: "Somebody's drowning!" Very few cared, but I was one of the few who took notice. I disliked this dissociation. I looked at my watch (for a journalist must register facts) and ran out to a diving board, from where I could see the person drowning. He was lying at the bottom of the sea, six feet down. He was on his back, and his arms were swinging with the current.

I am far from being a hero and have never been a good swimmer, but I was upset that nobody cared. I jumped down to get to the person, but I could not get hold of him. He was too heavy. I took another deep breath and gave it one more chance. This time I got under him on the bottom of the sea, pulled him over my back and swam toward the light. Up. Further up. When we got to the surface, he started bleeding from his nose and ears because of the pressure he had been under. He was unconscious. And I thought that I had pulled a cadaver up.

Then, at long last, rescue appeared in the form of a rowboat with some competent men. They brought us ashore and we started administering artificial respiration. An ambulance with a doctor arrived, and after half an hour we saw a dim fog on a mirror held before his mouth. He was alive. He proved to be a young officer who had gone swimming after a big meal. He had a classic Danish name, Arild Hvitfeldt, and he was stationed at the Holbæk garrison. Overnight his parents came from Jutland. His commanding officer at the garrison proclaimed that I had saved the life of one of his officers and asked for a citation from the Carnegie Foundation for my deed. Co-signatures for the request for a citation came from my editor-in-chief and Holbæk's police chief.

There was no medal with the citation, but the sum of money I received was useful for my ensuing studies in the United States.

31

Some years later, this scene almost repeated itself when I fortunately saved another man from drowning at a beach near Tel Aviv. He was a British-born journalist by the name of Harry Arvay, whom I was to succeed in a major PR position in Tel Aviv. He had gone swimming off the Accadia Hotel beach when a strong undercurrent pulled him out to sea. Like in Denmark, nobody seemed to care. Nobody comforted his wife and two young daughters, who were helplessly watching their husband/father being swept out on the whitish waves.

"You cannot look this little family straight in the eye if Harry drowns," I said to myself, mobilizing some extra strength. Again I thought something like "I am my brother's keeper" and entered the water to try to save him, although I was still far from being a good swimmer. But I got out to Harry, and heard him shout: "Clutch me!"

Then he went down – once, twice. I knew that a third time would be for good. I got close to him, pulled him up on my back and started moving toward land. Then a miracle happened. A wave, which I call friendly, came and pushed us closer to land. I could start breathing without taking in water.

A chain of people came toward us from the shore and brought us safely to dry land. Again the same situation, with an ambulance and a return to life. Harry later presented me with a copper vase with the inscription: "To Richard Oestermann, in remembrance of 18.8.1961 when you risked your life to save mine."

Studies in the United States

I got to the United States in a rather special way. For two years I worked in Holbæk as a journalist, but I wanted to get out into the world and learn more. Luckily enough, in Copenhagen I met a young American diplomat, Richard Trudeau, who was so happy with his journalistic education at the University of Washington, Seattle, that he persuaded young Danish journalists to follow suit. I sent an application to the university and received a scholarship for a year's stay. Seattle is on the other side of the globe from Denmark. How could I, a twenty-one-year-old journalist, finance this?

I sold everything I owned, including a fancy radio, and added the sum of money I had received from the Carnegie Foundation for having saved the man from drowning. And then the editor of my paper gave me an advance for six articles. "But I do not want to have these articles right away," he said. "Wait some months. Otherwise you might place the United States way up, where it does not belong, or way down, where it does not belong either." Good advice.

My year of study in the United States proved to be better than I had thought. Not only did we learn to write articles for newspapers and magazines, while always having the reader in mind, we also learned how to sell an article. American pragmatism.

By accident I discovered how good it is to be a journalist, not only for one country, Denmark, but also for Sweden and Norway. This was my own invention.

The year 1948, when I was in Seattle, was when the Olympic Games were held in London for the first time since the war. I had gotten to know the foremost swimming trainer of the university, and he was about to send his champion swimmers to London to harvest medals.

The University of Washington had some of the finest American swimmers at that time. This trainer knew the clocking-in times of all his swimmers by heart. And he also knew the times of Danish, Swedish and Norwegian swimmers. Among the American swimmers was Brenda

Helser, and among the Danish Ragnhild Hveger and Karen Margrethe Jacobsen.

Our talk turned into an article. Or rather three, with the same content, but a different lead for each of the three countries. I sent my article to *Idrætsmanden* in Denmark, *Sportsmanden* in Norway and *Idrottsmanden* in Sweden. Some weeks later I received a clipping from all three papers. They had used my story. I even received a fee for it.

So I learned something about gathering the Nordic countries. All of a sudden I had not one outlet, but three in one go. As a free tip to my colleagues, I will state here that I have successfully used this method for years.

I had regarded the University of Washington as a liberal place, but that proved not to be the case with regard to the Democratic politician Henry Wallace. The university would not let the politician speak to the students on campus, but only allowed him to talk, standing on a truck with a microphone, from outside the university area.

The next long tour I took went south, over Hollywood, deep down into Mexico, where I worked on a farm. This was the time of the Cold War. And time to chase Communists in a right-leaning USA.

During this period I had no connection with the Middle East. That only began when I learned that a Jewish state had been created after being attacked by Arab countries. The news about what had happened in the Middle East reached me in the wilderness of Alaska. Had I known more, I would in all likelihood have returned to join the group of Danish volunteers who had gone to Israel to fight for the state's independence.

But all this is theory. The reality was that I went back from the United States to Denmark and obtained employment as a journalist, first at the newspaper *København*, then at *Information* – a former underground paper that had surfaced to become a real newspaper.

One of *Information*'s chief editors was the resistance movement leader Børge Outze; the other one was Erik Seidenfaden, also from the resistance movement. They led a liberal newspaper with a daring course. Though only twenty-two years old, I had to cover the academic world and was responsible for the makeup of the paper – except the front page, which was the chief editor's domain.

Outze was known throughout Denmark for his editorials. They may not have been very deep, but they distinguished themselves by being written in the most beautiful Danish at the time. When Outze started writing the editorial of the day, we heard the sound of the typewriter being opened in his office, and then it was like hearing a machine gun for the next ten minutes until he left his room and let his manuscript descend upon us. He was great.

Therapy

When I look back on a long life in the press, I rejoice that I chose this profession. I am still writing for Scandinavian papers, every day – one, two, now and then three stories – relating to the Middle East. This is what keeps me going. Plain therapy. I have turned my hobby into something lucrative. Still, at eighty-eight and not healthy, I keep this up. And – lo and behold – some time ago I received a raise from my paper in Norway. What recognition. How many people at the age of eighty-eight can pride themselves on a raise in salary?

1958–1967:

From Israel's Tenth Anniversary to the Six-day War

Cyprus

In May 1958 Israel was going to celebrate its tenth anniversary, and I was burning to go to the Middle East as a correspondent. Fortunately, I was sent by Danish, Norwegian and Swedish papers to cover the festivities. I set out for the region with a stop en route in Cyprus, where a war was going on between Greeks and Turks, with the Brits on the sideline.

In those days one needed a British visa to go to Cyprus. When, in the spring of 1958, I discovered that it might take months to obtain such a visa, I applied for one right away.

British soldiers keeping a watchful eye on Cypriot crowd

In Nicosia all sides tried to get me to see the situation with their eyes. They took turns contacting me to schedule meetings where they would present me with their side of the story. I was pressed, but withstood all attempts of manipulation. The British information chief was Reginald

Storrs, son of the (acting) British high commissioner for then Palestine, Sir Ronald Storrs. I remember Reginald as a flexible person with good relations with both Greeks and Turks.

When I arrived in Nicosia, the name of its main road, Ledra Street, had been changed to "Murder Mile." The term was justified, because dozens of killings were committed there, in broad daylight. I toured the island with various groups. One of them pointed out a bay where four men had been shot down; another guide showed me where at least twelve men had been murdered.

The Greeks and the Turks were fighting over sovereignty of the little British colonial island. When I was there, the atmosphere was hectic, tense – and hesitant. The situation was just as acute and dangerous for the West as in Algeria, as if a new balloon were about to burst. As is often the case with an underground movement, some elements would use the political situation as an excuse to commit gangster attacks. The situation had deteriorated to the point that "politically motivated" robberies and shootings were commonplace.

Aiming at Israel

My aim in the Middle East was above all Israel, and the celebration of its ten years as an independent state. We journalists drove in small cars from Tel Aviv up the narrow, curving roads to Jerusalem to cover the anniversary festivities. People sat on sidewalks behind ropes and waited to hail the Israeli army. The atmosphere was tense, as Jordan had protested an Israeli military presence in Jerusalem, but Prime Minister David Ben-Gurion ignored the protest and went through with the march.

In a combination of unrestrained joy and military vigilance, Israel entered its big ten-year anniversary on the Givat Ram campus of the Hebrew University, by far the largest public place in town. Dozens of tanks and other military vehicles were parked in straight lines, awaiting marching orders. But first the president, Yitzhak Ben-Zvi, needed to arrive at the large stadium. He was driven in an open black limousine, with soldiers on motorbikes in front and a mounted officer behind, with the president's banner. They came to the area where the military was placed.

Then a starting signal sounded – and all the vehicles in the stadium ignited their motors at precisely the same time with a roar and blue color exuding from their engines. The celebrations could begin.

President Yitzhak Ben-Zvi arriving in an open car for Israel's tenth anniversary celebration

41

Truman

The picture I took of Harry S Truman after my exclusive interview with him, December 1958.

All journalists have their best story. Here is mine. As a young journalist I had an exclusive interview with former president Harry S Truman at his office in the Truman Library in Kansas City. It was in December 1958, five years after he had left office.

I arrived with twenty-five questions, which I hoped he would manage to answer in the thirty minutes I was granted for an interview. However, before the interview began he wanted to inquire about Denmark's view on NATO, which Truman had helped organize. I looked at my watch and said: "I would very much like to answer your questions – but only after the interview. None of my readers are interested in what I have to tell you, but only in what you have to tell me."

Truman looked at me. "What nerve he has," he must have thought. But the thirty-third president of the United States swiftly reacted by asking his secretary to inform the senators and generals waiting in the anteroom that their meeting with him would be delayed by ten minutes.

When the interview was over, Truman had his turn, and I answered his questions about Denmark and NATO. Before we parted, I was allowed to take a picture, and I have a great smiling memento. Later, when I reached Los Angeles, I sent him two prints with a thank-you note. He responded by returning one of them to me with his autograph. It appeared that I had found a new magic formula.

Four years later this was put to a test. In September 1962, Israel's former prime minister David Ben-Gurion was scheduled to pay an official visit to Denmark. This was the year after I had come to Israel and I asked him for an exclusive interview some days before his departure to Copenhagen. At the interview I found myself sitting across from David Ben-Gurion in his office. "I would like to ask you some questions," he said. Immediately, I recalled my conversation with Mr. Truman and said, "With pleasure, but only after the interview because I have twenty-five questions and only thirty minutes. If your questions can wait until after our talk, it will be clear that you are in the same category as Truman." Ben-Gurion looked at me – probably sizing me up me as Truman had done. Commenting that the comparison with Truman sounded interesting, he agreed to be patient until the interview was over.

After answering my twenty-five questions he asked, in his very direct and personable way, "Tell me, what was your mother's maiden name?" I told him that my mother Gertrud was born Grün. "That was also my name before I became Ben-Gurion!" he said. "Then perhaps you are my long lost uncle David?" I quipped. Ben-Gurion laughed. From then on our talk became very informal.

Eighteen years went by. Yitzhak Shamir, Israel's foreign minister, was scheduled to pay an official visit to Denmark in June 1980. The Ministry of Foreign Affairs called and invited me to an interview and I readily accepted. I found myself across from Shamir one Friday afternoon. He began to question me and I remembered my magic formula. I explained that if he waited until our interview was over, he would be classed in the same category as Truman and Ben-Gurion. Shamir was astounded. I imagined what went through his mind. "Truman, Ben-Gurion and myself? What's the connection?" But he waited until the twenty-five questions were answered, and we had a good laugh together.

The Eichmann Trial

After several visits to Israel, I settled there in 1961 as a correspondent for Scandinavian papers. I had wanted to move to Israel for a number of years but only if I could continue working as a journalist. The opportunity opened up with the Eichmann trial.

There must have been six or seven hundred journalists at the trial, from all over the world. Almost all of them returned home after the trial. But a few, myself included, remained, fascinated by the fact that Israel as an embryo country had so much interesting copy. More seemed to happen there in one day than in Sweden in a whole year. I may be one of the last journalists from this group still in Israel.

The Eichmann trial was meant to scrutinize what had happened during the war and serve as an eye-opener for young Israelis.

April 11, 1961, was the start of the trial against Adolf Eichmann, the man who perhaps more than anyone else was responsible for history's most gruesome mass murders. The world's attention was focused on Bet Ha'am, the theater building located on Bezalel Street in Jerusalem. Here was one of the worst criminals in the history of mankind facing thirty-nine witnesses, survivors from the Nazi concentration camps. In the middle of the stage was a glass box containing Eichmann, with an Israeli policeman on either side. No bullets nor poisonous ampoules could pierce through the glass.

Almost a year had gone by since Eichmann had been seized in Argentina and taken to Israel, where he had been imprisoned in Haifa. There he had been interrogated daily by Israeli police, in the presence of his defense attorney, Robert Servatius.

The atmosphere was tense when the doors to the courtroom opened. This was the first time that the public, represented by the world press, saw Eichmann after he was caught. In the hall were hundreds of journalists, jurists and representatives of anti-Nazi organizations from all over the world.

Eichmann in glass box during the trial, April 1961

Thus began a difficult period in Israel. For weeks, the court heard from dozens of witnesses about horrors, sadism and death during the Nazi occupation in Europe. At one point, though, the trial focused on the Danish people's rescue of their Jews in October 1943. Here was a report about something completely different – as the Israeli press wrote: "the Danish heartwarming, unique, courageous and competent efforts against the Nazis."

Deeply moved, the audience, headed by the world press, listened to the witness report by the Danish-born Israeli Werner David Melchior. Melchior told the world of the Danish people's opposition to the Nazi attempt to wipe out the Jews in Denmark, describing the almost miraculous way in which Denmark's seven thousand Jews avoided being deported to German death camps and instead were brought to safety in Sweden. Copenhagen-born Werner Melchior, son of the renowned chief rabbi Marcus Melchior, was himself one of the Danish Jews who were saved from the Nazis. Now he was in Bet Ha'am to deliver his witness report. Point by point he described the development in German-occupied Denmark, where the overwhelming majority of Danes rebuffed Nazi attempts to start an anti-Semitic campaign.

While everybody in the courtroom was seemingly touched by this report, which shone in a dark and bestial cruelty, Eichmann did not react in his glass box. He made his usual diligent notes in the heap of documents in front of him. But the testimony must have angered him, reminding him that he never understood the Danes, who were "difficult and acted completely differently than most other people in Europe."

Before Eichmann's death by execution – the only one ever in Israel – the courage and competence of the Danes was undoubtedly one of his biggest riddles of the war.

Sworn to Obey

Unlike the gallery of Nazis who were accused at the Nuremberg trials, here only one man was in the dock. Yet his crimes seemed to be bigger than those of others. His judges were representatives of the Jewish people whom he had wanted to wipe out. Eichmann did not refute any of the accusations, but stressed that he as a soldier had sworn to obey orders, and this was all he had done. Eichmann said, "If I get sentenced, you must sentence every soldier in the field who obeys orders."

This was the old story again, about individual morality versus discipline. Eichmann's deeds made him an extreme example, but his story will always have a topical message. Israel chose to put an idea, personified in the man Eichmann, on trial. It was Nazi Germany that was in the dock with Eichmann.

Bet Ha'am had 750 seats. Everyone who was admitted was searched for weapons, except the judges. Four hundred and seventy four of the seats were reserved for foreign and Israeli journalists, while the rest were for diplomats and official observers. In an adjoining building, Ratisbonne Hall, a former monastery, another 575 people could follow the court case on a large screen, as if they were in the courtroom itself. I was admitted to both places, but preferred Ratisbonne, as on the screen one could sense what was going on inside Eichmann when he got sharp questions. One could follow his lineament and the small movements around his mouth.

Years later, in November 2005, I learned much more about Eichmann by visiting a patrician villa by the name of Minoux in the Berlin suburb of Wannsee, where a conference of fifteen Nazi leaders had taken place on January 20, 1942. Eichmann was among the fifteen men who had sat around a large table and planned how they could systematically kill most of Europe's Jews, at that time eleven million people. Of these, six million died at the hands of the Nazis during the ensuing years, many of them gassed to death in German concentration camps.

I asked my German contacts if they had any idea how the cultured German people could join in killing Jews. Nobody could answer this question. However, my visit to the villa in Wannsee was not completely gloomy, as in many of the museum's rooms I found young German high school students writing down what they found.

While the Nazis had seen a solution of "the Jewish question," I saw here "the German question" in a new perspective – the young people wanted to delve into their country's gruesome history. A seventeen-year-old German girl, sitting on the floor with her friends and taking notes from the posters hanging on the wall, said to me: "I learn about the past of our people. It makes me sad."

Covering the Area

Following the Eichmann trial, I started writing for several Scandinavian papers as their Middle East correspondent.

It was and is challenging to be the eyes and ears of Nordic readers. At one time I wrote for some five Danish papers, as well as one in Norway, one in Sweden and one in Finland (Swedish language), with a total readership of just over one million.

My task is to synthesize what is happening. An editor in Scandinavia may receive the same story with different angles from Egypt, Lebanon, Syria and Jordan – a confusing mix. I would also receive these stories, and then it was up to me to try to turn all this copy into one meaningful story. The task included trying to explain what was happening in a levelheaded way, and to occasionally predict where things might lead. Not to take sides in the conflict. I had to represent my inquisitive readers and investigate situations on their behalf.

A great responsibility, almost frightening. Early on, I learned the truth of the old press dictum: "When in doubt – out." Do not write when you are not sure of the facts.

Deciding whether a story constitutes news or propaganda is also a journalistic task. In the end it depends on who is paying. If it's the sender, it may very well be propaganda. If it's the recipient who pays, it may be classified as news.

To begin with, some fifty years ago, I sent my copy by ordinary mail. Later we moved on to different methods of communication – ticker tape, phone calls, faxes and eventually e-mail. When my Swedish paper introduced e-mail communication they insisted that I use this method, which I did first reluctantly, then happily.

I was furious when, upon learning my age, my Swedish editor said, "You are fired! You are now too old for us." Silly. My Norwegian and Danish editors saw it differently. "It doesn't matter how old a journalist is," they said. "If he is in fairly good health, we will keep him. The older he is, the better he writes, and his connections increase with his seniority."

During a certain period, my paper in Sweden demanded that my copy should be in Swedish. I solved that problem by sending my Danish-language story to a Swedish friend in Jerusalem, a clergyman working as a guest professor at the Swedish Theological Institute, and he quickly translated it into Swedish for me.

I learned early on that some of the most valuable tools for a journalist are 1) a reliable watch, 2) a car that will start when ordered to and 3) a lot of physical stamina. Above all, a journalist must try to see a story from different perspectives. The coin always has two sides.

Before settling in Israel in 1961, I had visited Israel on behalf of Scandinavian newspapers already in 1955, when the state was only seven years old, and in 1958 to cover Israel's tenth anniversary celebrations. During those visits I wrote about the dedication of the Christian X Hospital for tuberculosis patients in Eitanim near Jerusalem – a gift from the Danish people to Israel – about the naming of a street in Petah Tikva after H. C. Andersen, about the Danish ship *Birgitte Toft*, which became a household word in Israel after it was the first vessel to sail through the Red Sea to Eilat – and about the enormous popularity of General Moshe Dayan.

In 1958, the chief of staff of UNTSO (United Nations Truce Supervision Organization) was the Danish general Vagn Bennike, who became one of several Scandinavian officers to head this organization for many years to come. In Denmark Bennike was known as General "Bang" in tribute to his leadership of the successful sabotage actions on the Jutland railroad line, which prevented German troops in Norway from using this route on their way to the sagging German western front during World War II.

In Israel it was rumored that Bennike was on the side of the Arabs in their conflict with the Israelis. This was never substantiated. But he was unpopular with the Israelis, as can be seen in a picture I took of Bennike and President Yitzhak Ben-Zvi, in which the Israeli head of state looks reservedly – to put it mildly – at Bennike.

Their reservation was not baseless. Soon after his return to Denmark he disclosed his position by joining the Danish-Arab Friendship Society.

Summoned to the Foreign Ministry

From the early years of the State of Israel, an intersection named "Kikar Shabbat" ("Sabbath Square") in downtown Jerusalem, near the ultra-Orthodox neighborhood of Mea Shearim, was a site of friction between religious and secular Jews over issues of Sabbath observance. Mass demonstrations of religious Jews against cars driving in this area on Sabbath turned violent, as stone-throwing demonstrators were dispersed by police, often on horseback.

The clashes between the two sides intensified from week to week and resulted in detailed coverage by the press.

I also wrote about this recurring drama, but one day I was summoned to the Foreign Ministry, where an official told me that the Israeli embassy in Oslo had reported back to the Foreign Office about my article.

"We would like you to write differently, more pro-Israeli," the official said.

"No way," I said. "I write about undeniable facts. This is known all over in Israel, so why not abroad?" I added that I would not take sides, and that my job was to write truthfully about what I saw. I am not a propagandist.

After this defense of the free press, I was not summoned again to the Foreign Ministry for my writing.

The Space Club

While the Eichmann trial was still going on, in July 1961 Israel seemingly changed the situation in the Middle East overnight by sending its first rocket into space, "Shavit II" (Comet II). I was one of the journalists invited to the launching pad on the Mediterranean coast, where we saw the rocket take off. The dignitaries present included Prime Minister David Ben-Gurion, Deputy Defense Minister Shimon Peres, director general of the defense ministry Asher Ben-Natan and the commander in chief of the Israeli Defense Forces, General Tzvi Tzur.

"The spectacular, successful launch," Ben-Gurion said then, "may have an importance far beyond the scientific achievement and may contribute to a more stable situation in the Middle East."

In Israel, the first reaction to this achievement was overwhelming enthusiasm. Israel was now, almost miraculously, a member of the great powers' international "space research club." Dozens of newborn babies in Israel got the name "Shavit."

The Israelis were ecstatic. Their rocket had been designed, built and launched solely by Israeli scientists and technicians. And the young state – with only two million inhabitants at the time and few natural resources – was the first small country admitted into the distinguished "club," which until then had comprised only the United States, the Soviet Union, England, France, Italy and Japan. Very few had thought of the possibility of a countdown in Hebrew.

News about the launch was still fresh when it was realized in Israel and the world that Israel had strengthened its position from one day to the next and added to its international prestige. The political importance of the rocket's deterrence vis-à-vis the Arab countries, which threatened to eradicate Israel, was enormous; it was hoped that we were one step closer to peace.

If the news about the rocket took the West by surprise, in the Arab world it was received with some fear that it might hold military potential.

Denmark Square
in Jerusalem

In the beginning of 1962, Israel honored Denmark by naming a large square in Jerusalem "Denmark Square." It is situated in the suburb of Bet Hakerem. The inauguration of Denmark Square coincided with the state visit to Israel of Denmark's prime minister Viggo Kampmann, only the second European head of government to come here after the visit of the Norwegian prime minister Einar Gerhardsen.

One of the speakers at the inauguration ceremony was David Ben-Gurion, showing the importance Israel attached to the great Danish rescue operation. Other speakers were Jerusalem's mayor, Mordechai Ish-Shalom; the former ambassador to Great Britain, Gideon Rafael; and Denmark's ambassador to Israel, Sigvald Kristensen. I too was honored to speak, on behalf of Danish Jews in Israel.

Ambassador Kristensen made a deplorable faux pas – he spoke in German. He had picked up the language while serving as ambassador in Austria. His English was poor, so he preferred to address the audience in German. A hush was heard. The audience was clearly shocked. How could Denmark's representative choose to speak German to Jews only some years after the Holocaust? It was an insult.

At that time, between 1961 and 1965, I was a correspondent for the liberal newspaper *Politiken* and it therefore fell to me to write about the event. I was in a quandary: if I wrote that Denmark's ambassador had spoken German, he might be reprimanded, called home and perhaps lose his job. I had only myself to consult on this matter. I decided not to write this important detail, as it might cost him his livelihood, and that was not for me to get involved in.

Still today I debate with myself whether I was right. Colleagues of mine to whom I have presented the dilemma believe I made the right decision. I will add a perhaps. I may be a hard-boiled journalist in many respects, but in this case I was soft. Yet I do not regret it.

Besekow Directs in Hebrew

In those days one of the greatest names in the Scandinavian world of theater was the Danish-Jewish director Sam Besekow. He flew almost two thousand miles to set up Bertolt Brecht's *Galileo Galilei* at Cameri, Tel Aviv's modern avant-garde theater.

It became one of Besekow's most difficult tasks. Firstly, because there were only five weeks between the first reading rehearsal and the premiere, and secondly, because it was to be performed in Hebrew, like all other plays in Israel, and his Hebrew was practically nonexistent.

This great theater personality, who in Denmark and the rest of Scandinavia was termed a stage phenomenon, or even a genius, had also captivated the Israeli world of theater, where he was regarded as one of Europe's greatest directors. Only rarely would Israeli actors be directed by a giant such as Besekow. For a Danish theater director, five weeks of rehearsals is an absolute minimum. In Israel that is the standard.

I was invited to rehearsals, but admonished to sit quietly in a corner. Besekow would often lecture his actors along these lines:

> The words will be right when we have internalized the play with our hearts and our minds. First, we must understand what the author had in mind when he wrote the piece. Then the part will gain meaning, and we will be able to express it in words. Once this is done it is my task to listen to the flow of the words.

In between rehearsals Besekow had hour-long meetings with the actors, in which he tried to give them an understanding of what was behind the words. The actors were taken by Besekow's enthusiasm, dynamic imagination and deep knowledge of theater.

I had known Sam Besekow and his wife, actress Henny Krause, for years back in Copenhagen. During his stay in Tel Aviv he told me that Brecht had presented him with *Galileo Galilei* during the playwright's stay in the Danish provincial town of Kerteminde in 1937.

A Talk with Ben-Gurion

In the early sixties everyone was talking about Prime Minister David Ben-Gurion as one of the greatest leaders of the Jewish people in modern times. In critical situations the nation supported his politics.

David Ben-Gurion, Israel's Grand Old Man

I had an exclusive interview with him in August 1962, before he was to go to Denmark and the rest of Scandinavia on state visits. We met in the defense ministry in Tel Aviv, as at the time Ben-Gurion was also the defense minister.

One of the topics we discussed was Israel's plan of bringing water from the Jordan River all the way down to the thirsty Negev Desert. He said: "The plan will be carried through. Let nobody be mistaken about it. If the Arabs attack us, we will counter them. Although the Arabs are stronger in words than in deed, we must be prepared for an attack."

Here Ben-Gurion used his hands to accentuate his words. He rarely
used gestures, but when it came to vital matters such as water, his hands
supported his words. He also used his hands to emphasize what he told
me: "If the Arabs offer peace, I will cancel my visit to Scandinavia. But I
expect to be in Copenhagen before that happens."

When I met Ben-Gurion he was seventy-six and he had, except
for one year, been his nation's head of government and defense minister
since the establishment of the state in 1948. He divided his time equally
between his two positions – during the first part of the week he worked
as head of government, in the last part he was defense minister.

His well-known mane of hair had gotten thinner, the lines in his
face somewhat deeper. But his movements were agile, and his whole
body radiated vitality and spirit. He told me that he believed that it was
decisively important for Israel that he be physically strong. When he was
in Jerusalem, he told me, he walked about three miles a day, and when he
was in his kibbutz, Sde Boker, he participated in the general agricultural
work. He kept in shape, he said, by walking and doing gymnastic exer-
cises, one of which was standing on his head. "It all strengthens nerves
and muscles," he said.

When asked what Israel's position in the Middle East might be in
ten years, he answered: "I am convinced that Israel will become the edu-
cational center of the Middle East, which it already is for many countries
in Africa and Asia. I will work for Israel to have a free high school and
university education during the next fifteen years. Compulsory education should be from the age of three to twenty-three, in order for a street
sweeper to have a university education and the wherewithal to earn more
even than a professor."

I also asked him this crucial question: "Will the pioneering spirit
still be alive or perhaps even stronger than it was way back in another
twenty or fifty years?"

His answer: "When I came to this country from Poland many years
ago, that same day I heard that the pioneering spirit was dying out. But
Israel still has the sources that create this spirit – the security problems,
immigration, the challenges of becoming one people, cultivating the
desert and creating new forms of society."

At that time I was a correspondent for *Politiken*, and my goal in writing was for Danish readers to get a more balanced and inside view on what was happening in the young Jewish state.

Ben-Gurion told me that he had been in Denmark on a short visit to Copenhagen in 1945, and he still remembered two things in particular: Copenhagen's medieval beauty, as he put it, and the quantities of butter. He knew about the Danish cooperative movement and agriculture, and he also was aware that a Danish queen, Margrethe I, had been the ruler of the Nordic countries in medieval times.

Ben-Gurion was not an Orthodox Jew, but he knew more about the Jewish religion than most. He had a study circle of learned men who met regularly in his home to discuss difficult religious matters. He had a great knowledge of Greek philosophy and Buddhism, which he admired. This interest, in connection with his willfulness and sharp views, such as the task of Zionism at the time, gave him several enemies. But even his opponents acknowledged that he was a great leader of the state; according to many Jews he was the greatest leader since Moses – perhaps an exaggeration.

It is a fact, however, that without Ben-Gurion the State of Israel would hardly have been imaginable. His almost visionary ability to place Israel in the world and the Middle East, and to successfully steer this course, made him one of the greatest Jewish figures of the century. "He had the courage to proclaim the end of statelessness in our time and give us a country of our own," Nobel Prize winner S. Y. Agnon wrote about Ben-Gurion.

Ten months after my interview with Ben-Gurion, he decided to resign from his posts as prime minister and minister of defense. He also wanted to withdraw from the Knesset, but a delegation from his Mapai party convinced him that his withdrawal might be interpreted to mean that he had resigned completely from public life. Here Ben-Gurion gave in, declaring that he had not thought of letting his voters down. However, he was firm in his resignation as head of government. He went to live in his kibbutz Sde Boker in the Negev, to be a shepherd and write the history of Israel.

The Ben-Gurion epoch in Israel was definitely over, and with that an era in Israel's history.

Balancing in the Middle East

Tension was rising in the Middle East. Although the Arab countries realized that they were in no condition to start a new war against Israel, they insisted that a state of war still existed, though no active military actions could be performed for the time being. They tried to undermine Israel's legitimacy internationally in political, economic and other spheres, with Israel responding forcefully in order to show that it was able to defend itself.

At that time, Egypt's president Gamal Abdel Nasser rearmed his country after the defeat in the Sinai campaign by receiving a massive Soviet support in the form of missiles and fighter airplanes. Israel sized up its defense situation as it awaited the crushing assault that Nasser always talked about, while considering starting a defensive war before it was certain that an Egyptian attack would be launched.

The tension peaked while Ben-Gurion was still in Scandinavia.

Then the United States decided to deliver a number of Hawk missiles to Israel, the first non-NATO country to receive this weapon. It may sound paradoxical, but it is a fact that a weapon such as the Hawk missile in Israeli hands was necessary for maintaining peace.

Many Israelis had the notion that Nasser wanted to strike before the rainy season began. He had stated that Egypt had rockets that could reach places south of Beirut (meaning Israel), as well as Russian-built TU-16 jet bombers which could carry ten tons of destruction against which Israel had no answer.

Against this background of a changing military balance between Israel and the Arab states, the United States took steps to reestablish the status quo and counter the influence of Russian weapons in the Middle East.

In 1962 I wrote: "Washington took the unusual step of informing both Egypt and Israel of the pending delivery of the Hawk missiles, stressing their defensive character. The American decision was surely taken to stop an Egyptian attack and to keep the Israelis from repeating the Sinai campaign of 1956. At that time no one thought that Israel would start a defensive attack, although it was up against a wall. Today nobody is so sure, least of all the Americans."

This no-war-no-peace situation existed for no less than five tense years, until Israel broke out of what it believed was a beleaguered fortress and started the defensive Six-day War in 1967.

Like all the other people living here, I was under the daily influence of this constant tension. "How will this end?" we wondered.

Who Is a Jew

The ancient question "Who is a Jew" was clarified to a certain extent when the Brother Daniel case reached the Israeli Supreme Court. It was December 1962, and the case, which got world attention, was about a Jewish-born Carmelite monk who wanted to receive Israeli citizenship because of his Jewish descent.

He was born in 1912 in Mir, Poland, under the name Oswald Rufeisen. In 1942 he converted to Catholicism, after having been saved by Catholics from deportation. In his youth he was active in a Zionist organization in Poland and during the war he joined an anti-Nazi underground movement, where he helped save the lives of many Jews. He came to Israel in 1959. For three years he lived as a monk in the Stella Maris Monastery in Haifa.

A few hours before the judgment, I asked Brother Daniel what he would do if the decision was against him. He must have thought that the judgment would in fact be negative, as he quickly answered that in that case he would apply for citizenship in a normal way.

The court case, which lasted only one day, was attended by foreign diplomats, Christian church leaders, many missionaries and some twenty members of various "Jewish-Christian" and "Jewish-Messianic" groups. Brother Daniel arrived accompanied by several church dignitaries and two nuns. Before the beginning of the court session he prayed for the verdict to be in his favor. He prayed in Latin, I could hear.

Crucial matters were at stake. Brother Daniel had obtained permission from the Vatican to bring his case before the Supreme Court. In court he tried to achieve what the Catholic Church had strived to obtain for hundreds of years – to obliterate the historic differences between the religion of Moses and the religion of Jesus, in its Catholic form.

After the court ruled against Brother Daniel he said that it was a big disappointment to him. "I will not go against a court in my country," he told me. "But it is difficult for me now to resign myself to the fact that I do not belong to any people," he said. "I still want to remain in Israel, if my monastic order does not send me to another country."

I found a strong personality in Brother Daniel. He was small of stature, but courageous of mind. He was bespectacled, with a dark full beard. He was passionate about his cause and thought that he carried it on behalf of many others.

One of the outcomes of the judgment was that there were now clearer rules as to who might immigrate to Israel and claim automatic citizenship. Zionism cannot accept a distinction between Jewish religion and Jewish nationality. If this were the case, a continued immigration of Jews to Israel might stop, and Israel would have to face that the connection with Jews worldwide might be broken.

Since the Eichmann trial Israel had not experienced such a significant court case. It gained attention way beyond Israel and in the United States it was the story of the day on television and in the press.

The court case developed into something like a symposium on Jewish law, history and sociology, where both parties presented quotes and counter-quotes from the same sources. From the judgment it became clear that there is no such thing as Christian Judaism. A renegade Jew – according to Jewish law – is still regarded as a Jew in most respects. However, a Jew who has accepted another faith has cut himself off from the rest of the Jewish people and cannot demand its privileges. This was the first time an Israeli court acknowledged that the question of status can be decided outside the realm of Jewish law.

The case clarified the question of who qualifies as a Jew in the eyes of the state. The time-honored concept that a Jew is a person born to a Jewish mother had been expanded in 1959 through a directive from the Israeli government, stating that a Jew is a person who in good faith declares that he/she is a Jew and not a member of another religion. The law of return does not state anything about Jews who have converted to another religion, as it is believed that Jews in Israel – religious as well as irreligious and even anti-religious – do not regard Judaism as a religion but as a nationality without a religion.

Now the matter had been taken up again, from a different angle. The Brother Daniel case showed that Judaism is a religion as well as a nationality – a combination that was characteristic of other ancient peoples as well. The Jews may be the only ones in the world today to combine these two aspects. Were it not for that, Israel of today would hardly have existed.

According to a supposed majority opinion among the Jews of Israel, Brother Daniel could not be regarded as a Jew. He was considered a non-Jewish Israeli – just like other Christians, Muslims, Druze and Bahai adherents who possessed Israeli citizenship.

The many perspectives and weighty implications of the trial made covering the Brother Daniel case an exciting experience.

Pope Paul

One of the highlights of the following year, 1963, was the visit of Pope Paul VI, who came on a pilgrimage to Israel and Jordan. It was the first time in nineteen hundred years that a pope set foot on the soil of the Holy Land.

Peter, the first pope, left the land in 55 CE for Rome, where he died sometime between 64 and 67 CE. Pope Paul's visit broke with the Vatican decision that no church dignitary above bishop rank could visit Israel because of its opposition to an internationalization of Jerusalem. Paul followed the progressive and liberal line of his predecessor, John, and came to see his flock in this part of the Middle East.

We journalists were informed that for reasons of security we could only see Pope Paul at one of several places: the Jordan-Israel border crossing, Nazareth, Megiddo, the Franciscan basilica on Mount Tabor or other places holy to the Christians in northern Israel. I chose the Tabor mountain and waited several hours for the pope to arrive.

There was a lot of tension before his holiness appeared. Eventually, he crossed the border from Jordan driven by a Jordanian chauffeur.

In order to write the story I remember setting up my typewriter at the end of my station wagon, with the trunk open to create a makeshift desk. I gained considerable time by parking my car in reverse, so I could be one of the first among a large number of journalists to send the story off to Scandinavia. It does not matter how good your copy is if you cannot transmit it quickly to your paper. You lose out to the competitors. To this day I always park in reverse, even if it takes more time to park, in order to be fast on the move.

I had no chance to speak to the pope, but a ranking person in his entourage told me that the pope's visit would make many Orthodox Christians happy and perhaps bring more Christians back to the church. It would also play a significant part in the endeavors to improve the relationship between the Holy See and the Jews and advance a de jure recognition of Israel.

"Unpopular, but Respected"

General Odd Bull

The former Norwegian Air Force commander, General Odd Bull, became the sixth head of the United Nations Truce Supervision Organization (UNTSO) in Jerusalem and the third Scandinavian on this post, following Denmark's General Vagn Bennike and Sweden's General Carl von Horn.

Because of his position, which demanded a high level of neutrality, he refused to give interviews to the Arab and Israeli press and also to representatives of the world press, stationed in Jerusalem. But in 1965 he accepted me as the first journalist, representing Scandinavia, with whom he would talk.

For many years the situation on Israel's borders had hardly changed – it was a kind of trench warfare. The ceasefire agreements between Israel on one side and Egypt, Jordan, Syria and Lebanon on the other were signed in Rhodes in the spring of 1949, but the prospect of peace, the main idea behind the ceasefire agreements, faded away as a mirage in the desert. While practically all conflicts were settled after World War II, the situation in this part of the Middle East remained as ignitable as ever. A strong enough spark could have set fire not only to the two parties concerned, but the whole world.

General Bull came here as a fire marshal, but without any other tools than the authority of the UN, and with only a mandate of observing and reporting breach of ceasefire. He was well suited for the task. In 1956, he had been in Lebanon as chief of the UN observer corps, which was charged with monitoring the situation following the conflict with Syria and the ensuing American landing operation. General Bull remembered serving in Lebanon under "confusing circumstances," but it straightened itself out, he said – and in half a year it was all over. "It was one of the few UN tasks that got solved," he said.

Bull and I met in the UN headquarters in Jerusalem, at Government House – the large compound in no-man's-land where the British military governor once resided and gave the place this name. Outside the building was a parking lot with dozens of white cars, with "UN" painted in big black letters on their sides. Inside the building was a babel of different languages, particularly Danish, Swedish and Norwegian; over one-third of the UN observers were Scandinavians – a quota that still remains. The strong Scandinavian representation is attributed to the fact that the Nordic countries are said to be completely free of self-interests in the conflict and that the individual Scandinavian officers have been actively interested in the cause of the UN.

I asked Bull which characteristics he considered it important that the chief of the observer corps possess.

"They should have the same understanding of him on both sides of the border," he answered. "But it should not be because of his popularity, as that may be interpreted as an expression of weakness. He should rather be equally unpopular with both parties – but respected. He must appear in such a way that he can talk about a situation in a matter-of-fact way with both Arabs and Israelis."

"I must be strictly neutral," he stressed. "Nobody could wish anything else from me."

We talked about a certain episode in which Syrians shot at kibbutzim south of the Sea of Galilee – an area, which, according to the UN, is on Israeli territory and not in the demilitarized zone. According to Syria, Israeli circles regarded the episode as an attempt to provoke Israel to a sharp reaction in order to divert attention in Syria from political problems in the country.

"Whatever the reason," General Bull said, "I was confronted with establishing tranquility on the border. Quietness returned."

To what extent was this due to the Norwegian officer? Bull was modest or rather cautious when he talked about his role in stopping the shooting.

"I talked to both parties several times," he said. "It became quiet, but I cannot assume the honor for this. It should be given to UNTSO's usual machinery, i.e., observatory and rapport activities."

Interviewing Sophia Loren

Some fifty years have gone by since I had an exclusive interview with the Italian actress Sophia Loren.

For one reason or other, she selected me from a list of foreign correspondents who had requested a talk with the great actress. I met her in Haifa during her filming of *Judith*, based upon the successful British author Lawrence Durrell's script, written with a role for Sophia Loren in mind. The plot was about a Jewish refugee girl who illegally reached the British mandatory land of Palestine. Her main coactors were the British actor Jack Hawkins, playing a British officer, and the Australian Peter Finch who played the secretary in the kibbutz to which she came.

They were both in love with Judith.

Every morning at five she would wake up in her elegant hotel suite and dress in a faded khaki uniform. She would then be driven thirty miles to the place where the movie was made. Filming started at 7:00 a.m. sharp. No excuses for being late.

It cost $4 million to produce the movie, and it was rumored that Sophia Loren received $1 million for her role. In my interview with her she would neither confirm nor deny this amount, which was a huge sum for Israel at the time.

This world-famous star – winner of an Oscar for her role in the Hollywood movie *Two Women* – came to Israel in early summer and remained until filming ended in the fall. Her stay was interrupted by short visits to Italy to meet her husband, movie director Carlo Ponti. He was jealous of all men and would not leave her out of sight. I remember being perplexed at seeing him sitting next to his diva wife during the interview (note Ponti's elbow in the picture of Loren and myself).

The plot of *Judith* was something of an Israeli version of a western. It was about a young Jewish girl who had survived the Nazi atrocities and wanted to create a new existence in Israel, in a kibbutz in the Galilee. The filming created a political ruckus, with the Arabs threatening to boycott

Interviewing Sophia Loren – the elbow on the left is Carlo Ponti's

all Sophia Loren movies in Arab countries if *Judith* would be regarded as "furthering Israel or Zionism."

Loren did not want to discuss politics, but she did not mind telling her age. She was thirty, but looked considerably younger. Her famous curves made the same impression on men as when she was in her early twenties. She was breathtaking with her beautiful chestnut-colored hair, lively green eyes and fast, quick-witted repartees, which disclosed her Neapolitan background. A major feature was her height – five feet eight – along with her almost masculine wide shoulders and her sharp cheekbones. What beauty; all of it wrapped up in one person.

She told me that she could not imagine being a "real" actress, because – as she said – "I am rather bashful and shy and could not envisage facing an audience." Asked how she managed the daily transition from her hotel luxury suite to the despairing, lonely Judith, she said: "I was just like Judith during my childhood in the village of Pozzuli near Naples. I feel completely at ease with this role."

There is little now to remind one of the thin, lanky girl who once had the nickname "Stecchetta" (spindleshanks) and whose last name was not Loren but Scicolone. "But," as she said, "then I stopped growing in height and began expanding in more interesting directions."

At one point during the filming her life was in danger. She told me that she had been sitting on a tractor, all alone, and she accidentally loosened the handbrake. The tractor started rolling down a slope, and she shouted for help. The owner of the tractor heard her cries and ran after his vehicle. He threw himself onto the driver's seat and stopped the tractor, seconds before it would have turned over. She was lucky to only get a scratch and could continue the movie shoot.

The part of Judith was made for her. With her warm womanliness she was able to give over how much Judith had gone through. She behaved with a delightful naturalness – she gave her interview without a press secretary, unlike most celebrities. But she could also play the great lady. "I do not play Judith because of the fee," she said. "I chose to act in this movie because I liked the role. For me it is not quantity but quality that counts."

"Can you identify with Judith?" I asked her.

"I try," she answered. "Judith is different from all other roles I have had. I have never before tried to play a Jewess. I love her strong personality. If she has set herself a goal, she does not give up. At the same time she is amusing, festive and full of pep."

I found Sophia to be quite a personality herself. She told me that when she was not filming she liked to cook – in a kitchen, which the hotel had established for her in her suite. She liked to read, she told me, and her favorite author is Chekhov. She seemed to be a perfectionist, completely concentrated on her role every day until late afternoon. And the next morning the alarm clock would wake her up at 5:00 a.m. – time to go to work. Sophia Loren did not achieve fame by sleeping.

Found Her Grandmother's Concentration Camp Card

I met the glamorous Danish actress Helle Virkner, married to Danish prime minister Jens Otto Krag, on her husband's state visit to Israel back in January 1965. Helle and I had been friends in our early teens in Copenhagen – we used to have lots of fun shooting paper bullets at each other with rubber slings. I followed Helle's later career as a most admired actress, her secret wedding to Krag in Nice on the French Riviera and her later fame as the wife of the statesman who coined the phrase: "I have a point of view until I take another."

Talking to Danish actress Helle Virkner, wife of Danish Prime Minister Jens Otto Krag, Jerusalem 1965

Now the couple was in Israel. I accompanied them when they visited Yad Vashem, the Holocaust memorial center. There I discovered something that I thought might be of special interest to Helle Virkner – an index card in the department for documentary material of those who perished – and I pulled it out for her to see. The card was written in Danish, and Helle Virkner burst out, deeply moved: "It is my grandmother's concentration camp card."

She told the entourage that the text referred to a Red Cross package, which was to be sent to her grandmother, G. Lotinga, in the Theresienstadt concentration camp. Ms. Lotinga was seventy-two years old when she was deported from Denmark to the concentration camp. She returned to Denmark after the war and died soon after.

Prime Minister Krag and his wife had difficulty holding back their emotions as they were shown around the Holocaust center.

Agnon's Overcoat

When the great Israeli author, Shmuel Yosef ("Shai") Agnon, received the Nobel prize in literature in October 1966, he was seventy-eight.

We lived near each other in the Jerusalem neighborhood of Talpiot, and knew one another quite well. We took turns hosting each other in our respective gardens. We would talk about everything and nothing. We met for the interview in his garden, where he received me in his usual attire – a short-sleeved, open shirt, with a black skullcap on his head, traditional for Orthodox Jews.

Shai Agnon, winner of the Nobel Prize in Literature

Israel's population was immensely proud of Agnon's achievement. They felt as if the prize had been bestowed upon themselves. The prize was an encouragement at a time when Israel was in a difficult situation in the UN Security Council vis-à-vis the Arab countries.

Israel was gripped by Agnon fever, but Agnon was modesty itself. I found in him a kind, dignified and humorous personality. He told me that what really bothered him was that so relatively few people in Israel read him, because they did not understand Hebrew well enough. "Hebrew writers are in a difficult, almost tragic situation," he said to me. "Only a few, even among the intellectuals, read authors like me."

About his plans for the future he said: "I want to express what God puts into my mouth."

The year before Agnon received the prize in literature, it was presented to the Soviet author Mikhail Sholokhov. Already then there were rumors about Agnon getting the prize. He told me then: "If I get the Nobel prize – good. And if I do not get it, well – also good."

He informed me that he had received six hundred congratulatory letters from all over the world. "They all deserve an answer," he said. Agnon was a literary giant, but a very modest man.

The large sum of money that went with the prize did not interest him at all. "I never cared about money," he said. His answer to my rather trite question about how he would spend the prize money was: "I cannot wear more than one overcoat."

A typical Agnon retort.

The Story of an Autodidact

Another literary event took place also in 1966, when Itamar Even-Zohar decided to translate Scandinavian literature directly into Hebrew because he felt that the works lost a lot of their quality from being retranslated from English, French, Russian or German. So without ever having set foot in any of the Scandinavian countries, he taught himself the Danish, Swedish, Norwegian and even Faroese languages.

According to Itamar, modern Scandinavian literature was one of the greatest and most important cultural influences in the world. "We [Israelis] would do ourselves a major favor by expanding our knowledge of Nordic authors and reducing the influence of Anglo-Saxon, mainly American, literature on Israeli culture," he said.

Itamar, who was twenty-seven at the time of the interview, was an MA student in literature at the Hebrew University of Jerusalem. He was a genuine pioneer in his field. It was a lingual and literary achievement to introduce Scandinavian literature to Israel in this way.

He told me that he had read Scandinavian authors such as Selma Lagerlöf, translated from English, French and Esperanto – but that he had to learn one or several Scandinavian languages in order to proceed in his quest. At that time there was nobody who could teach him any of the Scandinavian languages, and still he succeeded in learning the Scandinavian languages in the course of only two years, without ever having left Israel.

He started with acquiring Oxford University Press's *Teach Yourself Swedish*, and when he had learned that he went on to the other Scandinavian languages.

His goal was to publish an anthology in Hebrew of contemporary Scandinavian authors. He produced a book entitled *Sipurei Skandinavia* (Scandinavian stories), containing thirty-three short stories. It was a weighty anthology covering the period from the 1920s to our day. Sweden dominated with fourteen authors, followed by Norway with nine, Denmark with eight and the Faroe Islands with two. Itamar's book was launched in Jerusalem at an event that I had the pleasure of organizing, with the ambassadors of Norway, Denmark and Sweden in attendance. They all cheered his autodidact accomplishment.

He was interviewed by Swedish Radio, where his self-taught Swedish got attention. He gave the following reason for his interest in Scandinavian literature: "The Scandinavians in general do not appreciate their literature enough," he said. "They believe that only the so-called big countries have important literature. Precisely because I was born in Israel and raised with Hebrew as the only language, I understand that an important culture is not necessarily one created by nations with big populations. Scandinavian literature is now at least at the level of what has been written in other European languages. If Danish, Swedish and Norwegian were more widely disseminated, their literature might influence that of other countries and Nordic authors could become be an avant-garde in European literature."

Soon after our talk, he set out for the North to study the languages in their three respective countries.

The Saga of the
San Nicandro Jews

Just like Moses, Donato Manduzio never saw the Holy Land. He died before he achieved his goal. Still, he may be known for posterity as the prophet figure who motivated his people to leave their home and settle in the promised land, thus changing their fate.

Donato Manduzio's group numbered only twenty-three families – a total of ninety people who gave up their Catholic faith for Judaism in one of history's most unusual conversions. In 1949, one year after Israel's independence, Manduzio's followers left their birthplace, the village of San Nicandro in the heel of the Italian boot, and settled in the newly independent Israel, most of them in northern Galilee.

The story of this small community of simple farmers and their conversion to the Jewish faith is pieced together from sketchy historical facts, but it is viewed in a glorified light. With faces beaming with happiness, ecstatic voices and glowing eyes, this small community held out for years against difficult odds. They stuck to their new faith and were doggedly determined to become acknowledged as Jews.

The village of San Nicandro, situated far off the beaten track, near Mount Gargano, existed in obscurity and without contact with the outside world since it was established in the middle of the seventeenth century. It grew around the church, named for a highway robber by the name of Nicandro who in his old age presented part of his loot to the church and because of that was elevated to sainthood.

Nobody had heard about San Nicandro until Donato Manduzio accidentally came across the Old Testament in Italian and convinced a group of his fellow townsmen that this should be their Holy Writ and true teaching.

Donato Manduzio, although highly intelligent, had been an illiterate when he was seriously injured fighting for Italy during World War I.

While recuperating, a hospital nurse taught him to read. One day a street vendor from Naples sold him the Five Books of Moses, and from that day the saga of the San Nicandro Jews began.

This acknowledgment of the Five Books of Moses as being complete, without the New Testament, was denounced as heresy by the Catholic Church. The Italian fascist rule and the German occupying power looked askance at these new Jews. The leaders of the Jewish congregation in Rome did not look kindly upon the group either, believing that there must be something suspect in the fact that Italian Catholic farmers would voluntarily join a people as persecuted as the Jews. But Manduzio and his followers refused to be dissuaded.

I met the group in northern Israel in 1967, years after they had settled there. They looked and behaved like Israelis. Only a slight accent in their Hebrew revealed that they were not natives. I felt privileged to be meeting such devoted people.

Manduzio based his belief on the Jewish way of life, on the laws written in the Torah. Its agricultural regulations became incorporated into the daily life of these Italians. The Torah gave meaning to every aspect of their existence. It steered their lives, from cradle to grave, in stable and field, at home and within the community. Manduzio's small group never made a significant decision without first consulting the Bible. All this took place clandestinely in order not to challenge the authorities or suspicious townspeople.

At first Manduzio had only four adherents, but his congregation grew steadily. To begin with, they thought they were the only Children of Israel in the world. Even once they made contact with the Jewish community in Rome, many years went by before they became aware of the Jewish rebuilding of Palestine.

From the congregation in Rome, the San Nicandro community received prayer shawls and prayer books. Then the road was open to Hebraize the names of members of the San Nicandro congregation – Donato became Levi, Lorenzo was named David, Giaccomo changed his name to Amos, and Pietro to Isak. During the secret meetings of the congregation, a young girl named Rachel sat at Manduzio's feet and faithfully wrote down all his prophetic thoughts. I was fortunate to later meet

Rachel (formerly Maria) Leon and her son Elisha; by then eighty years old, Rachel lived in Biria, a village in the Upper Galilee.

She proudly showed me her notes, a bound book of some four-hundred handwritten pages. It contained Manduzio's diary, prophetic words and psalms – perhaps a gem for a publisher, who might want to publish a book on the saga of the San Nicandro Jews. "If my notes should ever be published as a book," Rachel Leon said to me, "I do not want to have anything added or subtracted. It must be as it is." I tried for months to find a suitable publisher in Scandinavia, but in vain.

In the beginning of the book Rachel Leon writes about the dark and foggy road that leads to the light of lights – not a simple story, but God's righteous words. Then she continues with the strange tale of these newly converted Jews.

An unusual event took place for the community when part of the Allied Forces went through their village in 1944. In that force was the Jewish Brigade, also known as the 178th Palestine Transport Company of the British Army. To the amazement of the Jewish group in San Nicandro, they had the Star of David sewn onto their uniforms. Manduzio's followers tried to get into contact with the troops, but did not succeed.

Then one of the members of the group had a bright idea – and during one long night the women sat sewing a huge Star of David flag out of two sheets and a blue evening dress. The next day the men stood by the roadside and held the flag up for the soldiers passing by to see. One of them noticed the flag and asked for a day's leave so he could return to San Nicandro to investigate.

It turned out to be a moving meeting, during which the soldier told Manduzio and his followers about the return of the Jews to the Holy Land and its rebuilding. Although this small community immediately decided to immigrate to Palestine, several years were taken up with formalities. Before their move the men were circumcised and the conversion of the congregation was officially acknowledged.

The next year Manduzio died, at sixty-three years of age. Even after his death his followers did not hesitate from achieving their goal. In 1949 the group went to Israel, where some settled in the village of Alma in the

Galilee, some went to the nearby village of Biria and others to Ashkelon in the south.

Elisha Leon, a businessman, is convinced that a divine providence steered his group to Israel. He said that today he is not a religious Jew. "I keep perhaps 10 percent of the 613 Jewish regulations. If I had kept them all – perhaps Messiah would have already come."

The Six-day War:
A Personal Perspective

Israel's victorious Six-day War (June 5–10, 1967) is still studied in military academies around the world. This was a turning point in Israel's history, from underdog to supremacy. However, this strengthening of Israel's position has carried a high price, with Israel being regarded as a kind of superpower without magnanimity toward its Arab neighbors.

The core of conflict, I believe, is that the Arabs, still reeling from being routed in consecutive wars, will not recognize Israel as a Jewish state, a homeland to Jews worldwide. They refuse to see Israel as a means toward improving their lot. Israel, for its part, with the United States at its side, is strong enough to test the goodwill of the Arabs, in the form of the so-called Arab Peace Initiative.

The Israelis maintain that they have nobody to talk to on the other side, that the Khartoum atmosphere with its three resounding nos to Israel still prevails. But times have changed since the Arab world in the Sudanese capital stated that there would be no talks with Israel, no negotiations and no recognition. Today there is somebody to talk to. The main question is the sincerity of both parties to proceed.

I felt the prelude to the Six-day War in various ways. At that time Israel was totally alone in the world. The Arab-Israel tension was rising, and came to the fore on April 7, when Israeli warplanes struck at Syrian artillery positions and downed six Soviet-built MIG jets that had been sent up to intercept the Israeli aircraft.

From then on it was all downhill. The Syrians complained that the Egyptians did not come to their rescue despite their defense pact. The following month, Egypt's president Gamal Abdel Nasser upped the ante by ordering the Tiran Strait closed and demanding that the UN observers along its borders should disappear.

Nasser proclaimed a closure of the strait to all shipping to and from Eilat. Israel felt that its existence was threatened. At one time there was talk about an international flotilla of ten ships that would break the blockade, but country after country backed out. The free passage of ships was stopped.

Israel was isolated. It was a nerve-racking period. "Send your children to us," friends in Scandinavia admonished my wife and myself. Our answer was a clear no. The Jews have run for thousands of years, now they are digging in. The Jerusalem municipality ordered garden owners to dig a trench in the ground for protection, as we had no real shelter. I had a villa with a garden in the Talpiot neighborhood and complied with the order – until I heard that Arab armies were now just a few miles away.

I mobilized my strength and said: "Stop digging. It is too easy for them. They can just shoot you in the neck. You are already in a grave." That may sound fatalistic, but it is actually what I thought. I also thought that if they wanted to get me, it should be in the house, where we would be behind closed shutters and where it would be more difficult to get to us. So we moved indoors.

The hero of our neighborhood was the local pharmacy owner by the name of Rubinstein. "I have enough anxiety pills for everybody for daytime use, and enough sleeping pills for the nights," he said.

On the evening before the war broke out, an Israeli officer, whom I knew as a librarian at the Jewish National and University Library, rang the doorbell. He told us that three tanks under his command were outside our garden and asked how he could drive them unseen along the road to reinforce forces in Kibbutz Ramat Rahel. "You will be seen by the Jordanian troops the whole way," I said. "The road is on a ridge." Later, I learned that in the darkness of the night the officer had managed to get the armored vehicles through.

About half a mile from our house was Government House, the UN headquarters. Jordanian troops had shown up at the eastern entrance and told the UN officers that they were taking over the building. The UN people could do little other than inform the UN headquarters in New York what was going on. With Government House on their hands, the Jordanians seemed to have an upper hand. If they proceeded to our neighborhood, Talpiot, they would have cut off an essential part of Jerusalem from the rest of the city and could claim a victory.

The war had not begun then, but it was imminent.

Then Israel started its defensive war. It struck across the Sinai border, while during the first sixteen hours of the war the Israeli Air Force destroyed four hundred Egyptian, Syrian and Jordanian planes, many on the ground.

It was an unbelievable feat.

During six days Israel routed three of its neighbors, who were themselves supported by several other Arab countries. Israel had captured or destroyed 500 tanks. Over 15,000 Egyptian soldiers were killed and 5,600 taken prisoner. Syria suffered about 1,000 casualties, and Jordan claimed to have lost about 6,000.

679 Israeli soldiers were killed and some 2,500 wounded.

In Talpiot life felt surreal. Jordan's King Hussein, in a telephone conversation with Nasser, said, "I also want to be in Tel Aviv this afternoon." Despite Israeli warnings to the king – via the UN in New York – about staying out of the war, the Jordanian monarch fired all the guns he had along the border with Israel. And the war was on in Jerusalem.

Our two boys, at that time four and seven years old, were in a local kindergarten and had to be taken home. My wife and I had their arms slung around our neck, clinging to us, as we jumped from tree to tree, in search of protection. We had not seen western movies in vain!

We had a guest over on the first night of the war. Lise Norup, wife of the Danish priest, had come over for coffee and ended up staying with us over twenty-four hours. The priest knew where she was because we had informed him by phone – the only means of communication that worked.

We were three grown-ups and two small children, trying to huddle under a Danish teakwood coffee table for some kind of protection. Our house was under attack, while the Israeli army retook Government House. I knew our house had been hit from the Jordanian side, because the next day I found a piece of a grenade in the wooden box with the children's toys. It had penetrated a steel shutter, ricocheted from wall to wall at the height of a child's eye, and finally landed in the toy box.

During the night I heard water gushing down into our backyard from a water tank on the roof, which had been hit. Soon the water would reach a jerry can of gasoline buried in the garden. "I have to rescue it," I said, and with bullets flying around me from the two armies, I managed to save the gasoline container before water reached it.

The next day, sitting not at my desk but under it, I could report to my Scandinavian newspapers that the war was almost over, that the Israeli Air Force was in charge in the skies, and much land had been taken. I was told by censorship in Tel Aviv that I could send only one story, that it had to be in English or French or German and that I could not answer any questions. I decided on English and dictated my story about the incredible victory to my newspaper in Norway, with a request that they should transmit it to Denmark and from there to Sweden. It worked. I covered my Scandinavian beat.

By the war's end, the Hashemite monarch lost half his kingdom. He had bet on the wrong horse. On a personal level, the war affected us socially – we had to cancel a dinner party to which we had invited some close friends. We had bought a duck for the occasion, and it waited all that time in the refrigerator. Then suddenly all electricity stopped. The duck was inedible.

On Thursday, June 8, the third day of the war, when the Israelis had just taken East Jerusalem with the Old City, there was a press tour to the Wailing Wall, now renamed the Western Wall. We journalists walked with the army through Lion's Gate on Via Dolorosa, until we came to the Temple Mount.

This was before the area was expanded into the vast Western Wall square; back then there were some low buildings in front of the wall. Upon reaching the wall Israel's president Zalman Shazar threw himself upon it, crying in happiness.

On my way out I saw a dead Jordanian soldier lying on the ground near the Old City wall. Nobody had removed the corpse.

For both Arabs in East Jerusalem and Israelis in West Jerusalem, the elimination of borders between the city's two parts was miraculous. They could again meet with old friends they had not been in contact with for years and see well-known places. During the next few years young people from West Jerusalem streamed to the bars of the Old City, and Arabs from the East saw their first supermarkets and other Western innovations.

It was almost too good to be true. Was it really reconciliation? If so, how long would it last?

I remember a conversation I had with a friend and tennis partner, South African–born journalist Philip Gillon, who said to me a few days after the war was over, "The Arabs can have it all back, in return for a real peace."

This peace still evades us.

On June 18 I was with thirty-five other correspondents on a tour of the Sinai. We had been flown in a military plane to Bir Gafgafa Air Base deep down in the Sinai, from where we went by bus to Kuneitra on the Suez Canal. Much of the road was full of burnt tanks and other military vehicles, and we had to detour through the sand. Here we saw the dramatic ending to the Six-day War.

I talked to some Egyptian soldiers who were trekking to the canal, mainly at night "in order not to use too much liquid." Among those I spoke with was Lieutenant Muhammed Said, twenty-seven, from Cairo, who told me that he and three of his fellow soldiers had been walking for six nights. He was barefoot. When I asked him about this, he explained, "Boots are too heavy in the sand." He was in good shape. In El Arish he had received water from the Bedouins. "I had to buy it," he said.

The tremendous victory made many Israelis arrogant. They felt that their country with just a few million inhabitants at the time had become a superpower, a feeling that came back to haunt them politically. They asked, "Would it have been better if we had said, 'Sorry we won the war?'"

Perhaps, deep down, many people would have liked Israel to be the loser.

In 1987, twenty years after the Six-day War, at a meeting of ten generals evaluating the war and its results, Yitzhak Rabin disclosed that Israel had taken an enormous risk when it sent two hundred of its airplanes to the defensive war against Egypt and Syria – only twelve planes had remained in the country.

Jew and Arab: Siamese Twins

Kalman Yaron at an international conference in Sonnenfeld, Germany, 1981

"The Palestinians and the Israelis are similar to inseparable Siamese twins – we can either live together in peace or kill each other."

With these words, the Israeli educator and peace activist Kalman Yaron summarized a penetrating interethnic dialogue that took place over a long weekend early in 1998 near the Ein Gedi oasis by the Dead Sea. A group of thirty-four Jews and Arabs held another animated meeting to discuss the bitter Israeli-Palestinian conflict. They exchanged ideas, unburdened their hearts and searched for means of coexistence.

Ein Gedi, where the group met, is a suitable place for contemplation and dialogue. It is an oasis in the Judean Desert, which has been a site of refuge since the time of David's flight from the wrath of King Saul. It is the isolated location to which the Essenes withdrew from civilization. Additionally, it is a healing resort for skin ailments.

The partners in this peculiar encounter were men and women from Israel and the Palestinian autonomous areas – a motley group of academics, public servants, educators and members of the staff of the Martin Buber Institute for Adult Education of the Hebrew University of Jerusalem. The participants conversed far into the night, in Hebrew and Arabic interspersed with English, expressing their thoughts and anxieties.

The same group had met before, in 1991, shortly after the Gulf War, during which the Palestinians had stood on their rooftops applauding the Iraqi Scud missiles streaking by, en route to Tel Aviv. At that meeting the Jewish participants denounced their Arab colleagues for this show of support at the anticipation of Israel's destruction, while their Palestinian fellows accusingly recounted Israeli cruelties against the Palestinians. However, now everyone seemed to be united by a true friendship that had grown and evolved over the years, diminishing their bitterness.

It was an irony of fate that the new Israeli-Palestinian encounter took place once more in Ein Gedi during an Iraqi crisis, and that the participants were still engaged with the same issue – anxiety about the possible use of Iraqi ballistic missiles against Israel. "It is good to meet again, remote from the outside world, to get in touch with our feelings," were the words with which Kalman Yaron opened the session. The participants, sitting in armchairs arranged in a circle, communicated passionately and tried to understand their interlocutors from the other side. One by one, almost all the participants took the floor and talked about themselves and their personal relationship with the other party, often very movingly.

For thirty years, Yaron – former director of the Buber Institute and chairman of the Israeli Multicultural Forum – endeavored to bring Jews and Arabs closer to each other, first by learning one another's languages and then through cultural and social contact. "We can choose our friends, but not our enemies," Yaron said. "Jews and Arabs must live together in this small land. There is no other solution. We each come here with our history and fate glued to us. We must speak to, not past, each other. Our mission is not impossible."

One of the most articulate among the Arab participants was television editor Mahmoud Abu-Bakr, who lives in East Jerusalem and is affiliated with Israeli TV's Arab sector. I talked with him during a break in the dialogue and asked him why there were demonstrations on the West Bank for Saddam Hussein – at the same time that many Arabs in that area prepared to protect their homes against a possible Iraqi missile attack. "It is the Iraqi people who suffer and for this reason so many in the Arab world side with Iraq, no matter whether a despot is the ruler in Baghdad or not," Abu-Bakr said. "And then there is another issue: Nobody wants Saddam to have weapons of mass destruction – but Israel still has such armaments. To many it seems like a double standard."

Asked whether he believes in peace between Israelis and Palestinians, Abu-Bakr answered in the affirmative and added: "I also believe in peace between Israel and the Arab countries, for the simple reason that everybody knows that both parties exist and will continue to do so, and that nobody in our world of today will be able to destroy the other group. No solution can be obtained with power. They know that also in Libya and Iraq. But unfortunately even if major changes have taken place in the Arab world, democracy is still not very common."

Kalman Yaron concluded the dialogue between the two parties by stating: "It is almost a miracle that two peoples, separated by blood and tears, are able to meet one another over a period of thirty years with love, without bitterness. It shows that it is possible to establish cultural islands, where an enemy is transformed into a friend. I have come to realize that living together begins with meeting one another. What took place here could not have happened in former Yugoslavia and not even in Ireland."

When the new history of Jerusalem is written, a chapter will probably focus on Kalman Yaron and his work in furthering an understanding between Arabs and Jews – Palestinians and Israelis. This special endeavor went way back, to the years before the Six-day War in 1967. Already in 1965 Yaron succeeded in establishing a night school for Arabs and Jews in the city of Ramla – situated approximately halfway between Jerusalem and Tel Aviv – where together they studied subjects of interest to them – from English literature to philosophy to the French language – not to obtain an academic degree, but simply to expand their horizons.

It was at that time that Yaron discovered his formula of getting adult Arabs and Jews to sit together on the same school bench. He used that experience when, shortly after the Six-day War, he opened parallel language courses in Arabic and Hebrew for the two groups. The courses were originally held at the Arab Al Rashdiye High School in East Jerusalem. Subsequently the French order of nuns, the Sisters of Zion, agreed to host the courses in their Ecce Homo convent on the Via Dolorosa in the Old City of Jerusalem; the courses are now held at the Buber Institute for Adult Education at Hebrew University's Mount Scopus campus. Yaron was a great builder of bridges between Jews and Arabs. His endeavors to bring the two people closer have, to a certain degree, succeeded not only in the Jerusalem area, but far into the West Bank, all the way to Hebron – the hothouse of Islamic radicals and fanatic Jewish settlers.

His efforts may be illustrated by the following events. Some years ago, when Israeli police and Palestinian demonstrators clashed near the Damascus Gate in Jerusalem, one of the Arabs said to his fellow demonstrators, looking at his watch, "Sorry, I have to leave you now, my Hebrew class is in ten minutes." Or as the late mother superior of Ecce Homo, Sorbonne-educated Mére Aline, once said at an Arab-Jewish gathering: "If we cannot have a big peace, let us at least create a small one."

The repeated setbacks to the Arab-Israeli peace initiative frustrated Yaron for years and years. Still, he was relatively optimistic. "There are major difficulties in the Israeli-Palestinian dialogue, and the reconciliation between the two peoples will not be easy, even after the implementation of the peace process," he said when I interviewed him. This peace activist believed that the violence that accompanies the journey to peace not only deepens the wounds between Israelis and Palestinians, but also produces a vicious circle of enmity and an irrational demand for revenge.

Kalman Yaron believed that the condition for solving a conflict is the willingness of both parties to acknowledge the legitimacy of the opponent and meet him face-to-face. With a quote by his mentor, the German-born Israeli philosopher Martin Buber, he explained that understanding cannot be achieved through technical communication but only by experiencing the other's identity, without losing one's own. Accepting is not the same as agreeing, as he put it. "By understanding the other's point of view, we may get a better insight into the other party, which may lead to a peaceful solution based upon compromise," Yaron said. He stressed that a dialogue with an opponent may be risky, because acceptance of the other part may lead to a weakening of one's own defenses, but "we cannot begin a dialogue without exposing ourselves to something unforeseeable."

Yaron also quoted Buber as saying that at the negotiation table clever diplomats, just like clever tradesmen, must weigh whether the advantages that can be attained through an agreement are worth the price. If the returns are higher than the losses, one must try the utmost to obtain a solution. Yaron believed that we needed Arab and Jewish peace tradesmen. This pragmatic approach was used during the Oslo negotiations between the PLO and Israel and led to a breakthrough in the relationship between Israel and the Palestinians.

According to Yaron, both parties eliminate historical facts that do not fit into their collective self-righteous self-image. While both Arabs and Jews remember the sufferings that were inflicted upon them, both are apt to forget the cruelties that they themselves committed against their opponents. Yaron's opinion was that unless these selective memories are revised, no Israeli-Palestinian reconciliation will ever be achieved. Both parties must be prepared to acknowledge that the road to peace will be full of provocations, hindrances and violent acts. The parties must accept the challenge to control their own aggressions and with all their power resist whoever wants to destroy the budding peace. And they must be encouraged not to give up hope for a better future.

As an example of the significance of communication, Yaron recounted an event that had taken place during an international conference in Tokyo when an Arab introduced himself to him.

"My name is Ahmad Hemda and I am from Iraq," he said.

"My name is Kalman Yaron and I am from Israel," was the answer.

The Arab appeared to be in shock. "I cannot talk to you until the Palestinian problem is solved," he said.

Yaron answered: "The Palestinian problem will not be solved until we talk together."

Kalman was one of the dearest friends I ever had. I share this sentiment with many Israelis and Arabs. He was known throughout the West Bank as the man who brought the two peoples closer to each other.

Kalman is no longer. He died some years ago. A great pedagogue, initiator and friend of many has gone.

UN Resolution 242

One of the most important decisions in the wake of the Six-day War was the adoption of UN Resolution 242, a tortuously negotiated compromise between competing proposals.

The resolution was adopted unanimously on November 22, 1967. It contains principles that have been the main guidelines for Middle East negotiations for forty-seven years – that "Israel shall withdraw its armed forces from territories in the recent conflict" and that "every state in the area has the right to live in peace with secure and recognized borders free from threats or acts of force."

Esther Herlitz, co-author of "242"

What only an inner circle knows is that 242 is a Danish invention. Esther Herlitz, a veteran Israeli diplomat, was Israel's ambassador to Denmark at the time. She told me the dramatic story behind 242:

"Denmark chaired the Security Council in the late summer of 1967. I was summoned to the office of Danish prime minister Jens Otto Krag. It was a late evening, around ten o'clock. Krag said that he intended to go to New York to make a speech at the UN. He asked me whether I thought that the Israeli government could accept the wordage that the countries in the Middle East are entitled to live within secure and recognized borders.

"It was too late to contact the government in Jerusalem, and so I took upon myself the responsibility of accepting this text on Israel's behalf. I believed it was a good definition of borders, and that it might have a chance of being accepted because the wording was vague enough to allow for multiple interpretations. The English representative to the Security Council, the late Lord Caradon, made a draft to the resolution and incorporated the Danish wordage of secure and recognized borders. However, some members of the Security Council wanted this sentence eliminated.

"Then I got a call from the head of the Israeli UN delegation, Ambassador Gideon Rafael, who wanted to ensure that this wordage be retained. It was past midnight and Krag was asleep in his summerhouse in Skiveren, in northern Jutland. His phone number was kept secret, but we overcame this obstacle by instructing a Danish-speaking secretary from the Israeli embassy to explain to the telephone operator the seriousness of the situation. She agreed to call him. Soon after Krag called and said that he would instruct Denmark's UN ambassador, Hans Tabor, to keep the text intact."

British diplomats later tried to steal the show from the Danes by calling 242 a British invention, but – Herlitz told me – it was established that it was cooked up by the Danes, with Israeli input.

For almost five decades, 242 has been the starting point and backbone of all of Israel's negotiations with the Arab world.

1968–1983:

Toward Peace with Egypt

On the Roof of a Burning Mosque

The date was August 21, 1969, and I was driving toward downtown Jerusalem from my home in Talpiot, when looking eastward I noticed smoke billowing out from somewhere high up. My professional curiosity steered me toward the Temple Mount, where I saw that the Al-Aqsa Mosque was on fire.

The Al-Aqsa Mosque

I parked my car and ran to the place. It looked like the fire was on the roof, and there were some ladders leading up to it for the fire brigade. I had no time to think of the danger – I knew I was on my way to a scoop.

I climbed up the ladder to the roof, only to find that another man of the press was already there – Rolf Kneller, a freelance press photographer. He took pictures and I wrote essentials down in my notebook. Around us was a flock of frenzied Arabs. When they started inquiring who we were and what we were doing, Rolf and I decided to descend. Perhaps the Arabs would have upset the ladders if they knew we were representing the foreign press.

We reached the ground and disappeared through the Old City alleyways.

The person who had started the fire was a religiously fanatic Australian sheepshearer by the name of Michael Dennis Rohan, who was arrested for the arson attack two days later. He was tried, found to be insane, hospitalized in a mental institution and later deported from Israel. In his insanity he claimed that he was "the Lord's emissary," acting upon divine instruction in accordance with the book of Zechariah. He said that he had tried to destroy the Al-Aqsa Mosque – the third holiest place in Islam, after Mecca and Medina – to enable the Jews of Israel to rebuild the Temple on the Temple Mount and thus hasten the second coming of Jesus as the Messiah to rule the world for one thousand years.

Rohan was alone in this action. Yet he set in motion a chain of anti-Jewish sentiment, with the Arab media accusing Israel of starting the fire. Rohan claimed that he had attempted to burn down the mosque after reading an article by Herbert W. Armstrong in a publication distributed by the Radio Church of God. Armstrong dropped his claims following the arson because at the time he was trying to establish a relationship with the government of Israel, as he had previously obtained a contact with King Hussein of Jordan before the Six-day War.

In October 1969, two months after the fire, I had an exclusive tour of the mosque to see the repairs. The Waqf had partially reopened the mosque and had begun repairs in order to negate the rumors, especially in the Arab world, that the mosque had "burned down." I was escorted by a Muslim official, Sheikh Ansari, who showed me three holes in the roof near the famous silver dome and the damage to the ornamented walls. Straw mats covered the floors, as the precious carpets had been stored away before the repairs began. The eight-hundred-year-old pulpit, presented by the Crusaders' slayer Saladin, had been destroyed by the fire.

At that time, already two-thirds of the mosque could be used for religious services. Some months later the repairs were complete and there was again a full house for the Friday prayers, with thousands of worshippers.

The Jesus Movie

I never saw the movie *Jesus Christ Superstar* – but I saw it being filmed. In December 1971 I traveled to Bet Guvrin, a mountainous area with many caves located in southern Israel, to talk with the movie's director, Norman Jewelson. The movie is based upon the rock opera about Jesus, which used music by Andrew Lloyd Webber and lyrics by Tim Rice. The opera was a major success, with performances in New York and Los Angeles.

Jewelson, known for having directed *Fiddler on the Roof*, told me that the movie did not presume to be biblical or historical. "It does not pretend to be authentic," he said. "We did this deliberately in order to show that the same might happen today." Some people called the project blasphemy, others said it was anti-Semitic, and that it would raise a storm. No doubt, it was a movie that would stir up emotions.

I met the actors. The role of Jesus was given to a twenty-nine-year-old American rock singer from Texas, Ted Neeley, of (red) Indian background, while Judah was played by a black actor and Maria by a girl from Hawaii. The group of young apostles surrounding Jesus was portrayed by Jewelson as an underground revolutionary movement during the Roman occupation of the land.

In order to make the movie, the Roman soldiers in it were equipped with the weapons of that time, and also with machine guns. There were scenes with tanks and warplanes.

Ted Neeley told me: "It is frightening to see how people react toward me as Jesus. After our performance in Los Angeles I was approached by a woman who handed her child to me and said, 'Bless him.' I could only tell her that I was an actor. I play Jesus as a man, but I cannot ignore the divine. I draw parallels between what I know about the time of Jesus and our own, seen through the eyes of a twenty-nine-year-old man."

Ted Neeley is a small, slight man with a reddish-blond full beard – hardly what one would have imagined as the typical Jesus. He was born in Ranger, Texas. His father – of Irish-English background – was an oil worker and his mother half Indian, of the Cherokee tribe. Originally he wanted to become a Baptist preacher, but after a period as a cowboy and bullfighter in a rodeo, he got his own band, which toured western United States. He competed with many for the role as JCS and had his breakthrough as Jesus when the rock opera was performed in Los Angeles. Earlier, he performed in *Hair* (as Claude) in New York and Los Angeles.

Most of the opera – and the movie – are told from Judas's perspective. Carl Anderson, a great American black actor, aged twenty-seven, was chosen to play Judas. He also played the role on Broadway and in Los Angeles. Anderson comes from a Baptist family in southern United States, has ten brothers and sisters, and used to be a jazz and rock musician. He too was chosen for the part from among hundreds of candidates.

The filming I witnessed was the beginning of Judas's death scene, after he discovers how harshly the authorities dealt with Jesus and is overcome by guilt at betraying him. "I do not know how I can love him," Carl Anderson sings about Jesus, after Jesus has been taken away to be crucified.

Judas's scene was filmed near Bethlehem in the artificial mountain of Herodion, where King Herod built one of his fortifications two thousand years ago. Carl Anderson played the scene intensely and dynamically, a great dramatic performance.

The man behind the movie, Norman Jewelson, is Canadian born and was originally a director of television programs. He first heard about JCS when he filmed *Fiddler* in Yugoslavia and cabled Universal Pictures in the United States to say that if they were thinking of making a movie of JCS, he was interested in directing it.

JCS was shot on location near Bethlehem, Jerusalem, the Dead Sea, the Sea of Galilee, Beersheba, Bet Guvrin and Nazareth. "What makes this movie different from the opera," Jewelson told me, "is that it is filmed in Israel, where Jesus wandered. I believe it will give a deeper understanding of Jesus and Judas."

Yom Kippur Interrupted by War

It was in the early afternoon on October 6, 1973, that the news about the joint Egyptian-Syrian attack reached our synagogue on Yom Kippur. The house of worship was full. Nobody had imagined that there would an attack on Israel at a time when the country would be paralyzed for twenty-five hours – without any public transportation, and with most of the population fasting.

From my seat in the synagogue I saw that two young men – to whom somebody had whispered something – had left in a hurry, soon to be followed by other physically fit men. We could hear a commotion outside. Cars started driving – on Yom Kippur!

I myself ran home as soon as I heard what was happening. There was no news on the radio or the television in conformity with the rules of the holy day. The whole neighborhood was in uproar. "Israel is being attacked!" sounded from man to man.

At that time I was the correspondent for Danish Radio. They contacted me and said they would get back to me in another few minutes for a live radio broadcast. I was going to be the first person to tell five million Danes that Israel had been attacked and that its fourth war had begun.

Let me admit it – I was quite tense, not only because of what had happened, but also because I was about to talk live, without any chance of correcting anything. "Easy, easy," my editor in Copenhagen said. "Take a piece of paper and write down what you want to say." My maiden appearance live went quite well. Now I was ready for anything.

The war developed quickly, much like the Six-day War, with an overwhelming Israeli victory. The Arabs, who called the war the "Ramadan War" or the "October War," started out quite successfully, but soon the Egyptians and the Syrians were routed. By the war's end Israeli artillery had Damascus within reach, and on the Egyptian front Israel was – almost – ready for a march on Cairo.

For some time before the Yom Kippur War broke out, it was clear to some Israelis that war was imminent. The Egyptians and the Syrians could not accept their defeat to Israel in the Six-day War and their loss of territory in the long run. The Arabs were looking for a way to avenge the humiliation of their defeat.

In the beginning of September 1973, major Israeli infantry, artillery and armored forces arrived at the borders with Lebanon and Syria. The Palestinian news bureau Wafa reported that an Israeli retaliation for terrorism against Israeli goals was very likely. At the end of the month the Syrians had moved a number of troops, which had been stationed for three years along the Jordanian-Syrian border, to the Golan front. In Israel this was perceived as a goodwill gesture to Jordan as part of a relaxation of tension between the two countries and a resumption of military cooperation between the three parties.

Just some days before, during the Jewish New Year, on September 27, Israeli forces on the Golan were reinforced. In Arab circles this was interpreted as a prelude to an Israeli attack, to counter the military build-up of Egypt, Syria and Jordan. However, the Israeli military move was in fact merely a routine practice during Jewish holidays. According to Israeli reports, Egypt opened fire at the Suez Canal and crossed it in several places, while Syria opened fire along the ceasefire lines on the Golan Heights. There were eighty-one Nordic military UN observers on the borders – thirty-three Swedish, twenty-five Finnish, twelve Danish and eleven Norwegian officers. I was friendly with some of them. They were positioned on all of the fronts, and I felt that they too would be in danger.

A highlight of the war was when Russian-made SAM missiles placed on the west side of the canal successfully started downing Israeli aircraft, one after the other. Israel had no answer to this in the beginning. The Egyptian success meant that the Egyptians might soon be able to move the missile positions still closer to Tel Aviv and that Israel's air force might bleed to death, which would result in Israel losing the war.

The Israelis had a real fright. What should they do? Wait until, perhaps, the American warplanes would have the same fate? The population was scared stiff. Many felt that doomsday was approaching.

The answer came from General Ariel Sharon, who decided to attack the missile batteries on the ground. He sent infantry, artillery and tanks to the other side of the canal. They did the job and eliminated the missile positions. The Israeli military was eighteen miles west of the canal, fifty-six miles from Cairo. The fortunes of war were with the Israelis again.

Sharon, then forty-five years of age, was the brain behind establishing this bridgehead, which became a decisive turning point. He was the former commander of Israel's famous military unit "Number 101," which carried out several retaliation actions in Arab neighboring countries before the Six-day War, and he commanded a major Israeli force in Sinai during the war. He had resigned as an active officer to become a conservative politician, but was recalled after the Egyptian-Syrian invasion.

After lying in a coma in an Israeli hospital for eight years, Sharon died in the beginning of 2014, thoroughly missed by a large part of Israel's population.

Fighting ceased on October 24, after eighteen days of intense warfare. On the east bank of the Suez Canal, Egyptian forces kept two bridgeheads for a depth of some six miles. The Israelis held over six hundred square miles of Egyptian land on the west bank. The Egyptian Third Army, surrounded by Israeli troops, totaled some twenty thousand troops and approximately three hundred tanks. The war was over on the Egyptian front. Israel's counterattack had earned the state a good bargaining position for future negotiations.

I vividly remember visiting Egypt at the war's end. Together with four other foreign correspondents and an escort officer from the Government Press Office, I drove my station wagon through Sinai and crossed the canal on a makeshift bridge – a primitive pontoon bridge, a hundred yards long and some six yards wide. We were in Africa, with its many palm trees, waterways, canals, camels and donkeys. People we met did not believe that the great Egyptian army had suffered such a defeat. They preferred not to talk about it. Still, we interviewed troops and saw the devastation.

In the late afternoon we crossed back to the eastern side to return to Jerusalem. It was beginning to get dark. All along the way, people from the kibbutzim had set up tables with snacks and drinks for the returning Israeli troops.

We still had several hundred miles to go when the car hit an obstacle
– perhaps an act of sabotage – and gasoline started running out of the gas
tank. As always in the desert, I had a jerry can with gasoline in reserve.
But now there was a hole in the tank – how were we to keep the precious
drops from disappearing? The answer came from an Israeli soldier, who
had hitched a ride with us from the Bir Gafgafa base.

"Does anyone have gum or a chocolate bar?" the soldier asked. He
got both, and then he turned the chewing gum into something like a screw,
wrapped it in aluminum paper from the chocolate bar – and crawled
under the car to place his invention in the hole.

"Pour in one liter," he said to me, holding the jerry can. Once he
had checked that the screw was holding up, I poured another liter in. We
restarted our journey. Every few miles we poured more gas from the can
into the tank. We drove slowly through the darkened desert. When we
came to the first gas station, its attendant looked at the screw admiringly
and gave us a full gas tank.

"If the screw has held until now, it will work for the rest of your trip
to Jerusalem," he said, and added: "It is perhaps with such improvisation
and inventiveness that Israel wins its wars." We managed to get back to
Jerusalem, where a car repair garage replaced the makeshift screw.

Another memory from the war was a visit to Kantara on the Suez
Canal, where we, to our amazement, saw people in pajamas in broad
daylight – only to learn that this was the general attire in that area – and
where in the streets of the war-torn city we saw cars and military trucks
piled on top of one another, as a result of the fighting. On the way to
Kantara – in addition to seeing the wreckages of tanks and trucks – we
saw only sand, sand and sand.

Before the war was over, it was clear that Israel's foremost goal – a
total defeat of the Arab invasion forces to prevent a repeat – could not be
attained. But that ambition gave way to a hope that Israel might be closer
to a peace with Egypt.

The war was a traumatic experience for Israel, not only because of
the fight itself against overwhelming odds, but also because of the lack
of protest and expressions of sympathy. An official in the Israeli Ministry
of Religion said: "The telephone is silent. None of our Christian friends

have come for a visit. I only remember one time earlier when it was so quiet here – during the Six-day War." In the midst of its stunning military victory, Israel felt abandoned and isolated.

Already on October 12, six days after being attacked, the Israelis believed that they were on their way to victory. "We are en route to Damascus," some Israelis said. But the cost was immense: 2,673 Israeli soldiers killed, 500 during the first week. Proportional to the American population, this would have meant about a quarter of a million fallen American soldiers in a little less than three weeks.

Again one witnessed the ironic turn of events: the Arabs who went to war to push the Israelis back, found that they themselves were driven backward. Israel actually accepted a ceasefire already on October 24, but the Egyptians chose to continue the war, possibly because the government in Cairo was not really aware of the military situation. Israel's leading military commentator, General (later president) Chaim Herzog, said that the Egyptians had placed themselves in "a world of fantasy" by not recognizing the Israeli conquests on the west bank of the canal.

Again the Arabs refused to reconcile themselves to Israel's existence.

Attrition and Watchman

During Egypt's War of Attrition against Israel (1968–1970) I remember running to the funerals of young men killed in that static encounter on the Suez Canal.

Every day the front pages of newspapers had five or six pictures of soldiers who had been killed the previous day, and I felt that I had to attend the burials of some of these young men, whom I either knew personally or who were sons of friends. A miserable period, which lasted for two years as an Egyptian prelude to the Yom Kippur War.

"Who were the casualties yesterday? Have they been identified?" people would ask hesitantly. The scene repeated itself, day after day, with people in mourning trying to comfort each other.

The name for the war was coined by Egyptian president Gamal Abdel Nasser. On June 23, 1969, Nasser said, "I cannot conquer the Sinai, but I can wear Israel out and break its spirit by attrition." Nasser felt that, eventually, Israel would be forced to withdraw from the canal.

Another war of attrition took place on the Syrian front in early 1974, after the Yom Kippur War. This Syria-initiated war was limited, but intensified from day to day, with Israel taking the attitude of passive resistance. This mini war did not make Israel give in, any more than the Egyptian one had. But Israelis who lived in the north felt the pressure, even though the fighting took place far from their homes.

For me personally it was one of the most difficult periods in my life. The tough situation was apparent in practically all homes in the country. Parents took turns patrolling their children's schools to prevent terrorist infiltration and to establish whether bombs had been placed on the school campus during the night.

For a long time, a forty-eight-year-old professor at the Hebrew University of Jerusalem had the task – equipped with a submachine gun and accompanied by a colleague – to comb the university campus on night patrols. On one particular night, he was out patrolling a few days after he had been on a three-hour guard duty at his son's school, and five days before he showed up for a four-hour guard duty at his daughter's school. A week later he was called up for military duty in the reserves of the army. His wife reported to a civilian night patrol in the streets of their neighborhood – armed, and escorted by a male colleague. One of the rules was that a married couple could not patrol together.

During this period the standard of living was lowered by 4-5 percent in order that Israel could continue to exist. Everybody accepted this burden. The morale was high.

Begin: "I Was Not a Terrorist"

Menachem Begin walked resolutely up and down the floor of his office in the Knesset. "I take these steps to emphasize my words," he said to me.

Menachem Begin in the zenith of his career

I believe I was the first foreign correspondent to interview the colorful rightwing leader before the forthcoming parliamentary elections in the spring of 1977. It was not difficult to get an interview with him. Nobody but himself and his followers thought that he would have a chance against the all-powerful Labor party, which had ruled Israel for the whole of the state's existence – twenty-nine years. All along, Begin had been patiently waiting his turn. He had a feeling that now it would be his time. He thought that the Israeli voters would nix Labor, that they would punish Labor for its misdeeds, and that he would now take over.

Begin paced up and down his office floor. He told me to put my tape recorder aside. "I will express myself so clearly, that you will realize that what counts is what I say directly to you, not through a machine," he said.

He was right. I almost felt that he dictated my story, paragraph by paragraph. There was no question that was too difficult for him to answer.

"Were you a terrorist?" I started out.

He immediately distanced himself from this term. "The simple fact is that we members of the Jewish underground fought to save a people from extinction and during this fight endeavored to avoid harming a civilian population," he said.

Begin was sixty-four when I interviewed him. According to an opinion poll, his party, the Likud, would be the largest after the Knesset election and obtain 36 of the Knesset's 120 seats, while the biggest party, Labor, would drop almost catastrophically from 50 to 33 mandates.

Begin won a sensational victory, obtaining forty-three seats, seven more than predicted. He became prime minister and a new era began in Israeli politics.

The term "terrorist" had been glued to Begin's name in the Arab world and in Great Britain since his Irgun group in 1948 had kidnapped and murdered two British sergeants in retaliation for the British execution of Jewish resistance men. Some people later saw the event as a forerunner of Arab hostage actions.

Begin denied this. "We did not use hostage methods," he said. "Those were used by brutal powers to kill innocent people. Our men were sentenced to death by the British authorities. We had told them beforehand that we would not tolerate hangings. If one of our men fell in fight, there would be no reason for us to take revenge. But those who were taken prisoners had to be dealt with in a civilized manner."

He went on: "Those who now, rightly, are called terrorists endeavor to destroy a people. They plan murders on women and children and are happy if they succeed. Any comparison between the Jewish freedom fighters and these terrorists is blasphemy. If one endangers one's life fighting for a just cause – that is not a hindrance to obtaining the confidence of the people and being democratically elected. In fact, it's just the opposite, as has been shown in many countries.

"We took hundreds of British officers and soldiers prisoner during the fighting and did not harm any of them." he said. "But the British government decided to hang our men to break the Jewish resistance."

Here Begin looked me straight in the eye and said: "The two British sergeants were soldiers, not civilians. If the British had not persisted in hanging our men in Acre prison, they would not have been harmed. We carried out the execution of the two sergeants with a heavy heart in order to save dozens of our freedom fighters from being hanged. It was an unavoidable retaliation to stop the British hangings, and our actions did just that." Begin told me that in a later correspondence with the father of one of the sergeants, a Mr. Price, Begin recommended that Mr. Price turn to Westminster and blame them for the act, which "we never wanted, but were forced to do in order to save human lives."

Begin was a controversial figure, a Polish-born Zionist leader, lawyer and orator, who, during World War II, was sent to work camps in Siberia, and in 1942 came to Palestine to become the head of the revisionist Zionist movement. He had since become one of the leaders of Israeli politics, but many people all over the world would get chills at the thought of Begin as prime minister.

"How realistic do you think your chances are of coming to power?" I asked him.

"It is time for a new government," he answered. "In much of the population there is a strong conviction that changes are necessary. Likud now has a chance of becoming the largest party."

"The foremost priority of a Likud government," he said, "would be to avoid a new war." He believed that a Likud government would deter aggression. "With such a government Israel could begin initiating peace via a friendly country, in order to have direct talks about a peace agreement," Begin said.

"The relationship to the United States should be built on reciprocity," he went on. "Israel helped the free world prevent the Middle East from becoming Communist – in return Israel deserves the help of the free world."

Begin denied that he was implacable toward the Arabs. "We are conciliatory," he said. "We want to live in peace and equality and obtain socioeconomic progress. We will give the Arabs freedom to choose their citizenship, cultural self-government and a humanistic solution to the refugee problem. But we will not put up with a destruction of our national security and expose our civilian population to enemy artillery fire and thereby miss the opportunity for peace in our generation."

"Will your politics and reputation not scare off Israel's friends, especially the United States?" was the final question.

"If the Israelis show confidence in us, our government will be able to further develop Israel's friendship with the United States, and Israel's true friends will become convinced of our cause," Begin said.

Sadat in Jerusalem

The eyes of the world were upon Jerusalem on November 18, 1977, when "Operation Sadat" began with the arrival of Egypt's president Anwar Sadat in Israel on his special peace mission.

Sadat wrote world history with his daring act. He had accepted Prime Minister Menachem Begin's invitation to come to Jerusalem and speak in the Knesset. We all hoped that a new era was about to begin. The excitement was enormous in Israel before the arrival of the country's archenemy. All over, Egyptian flags were hoisted.

Sadat decided to go to Israel for a number of reasons. He was impatient because of the lack of real progress in the Middle East negotiations, but he well knew that he had set unknown forces in motion. He believed that a major reason for the Arab-Israeli conflict was psychological, and that he had to unsettle the situation, to give it a shake, in order to proceed. In addition, Egypt was tired of fighting the wars of other Arab countries, and needed peace to bring down military costs. "No more war, no more bloodshed," was Sadat's famous slogan.

He received a royal welcome at the airport and came down the gangway to a red carpet, fanfares, a warm welcome by Begin and cheering Israelis as he arrived in Jerusalem.

He had executed his decision to come to Jerusalem with lightning speed, probably in order to prevent the formation of a major opposition to his trip on the home front and in the Arab world at large. He was undoubtedly supported in his mission by Saudi Arabia, but Libya, Syria, Iraq and Lebanon called him a traitor to the Arab cause.

I particularly remember one scene from his press conference with the foreign and local media. Security was so strict that the guards excluded one of Israel's veteran photographers. The poor man burst into tears. "How can you do this to me?" he said. "I have been waiting for this all my life."

Jerusalem was packed with hundreds of foreign journalists who had come to cover the event. We got close to Sadat several times, but were prevented from talking to him. Many of us had one thing in mind – to get as fast as possible to Cairo and see how the Egyptians were reacting to Sadat's daring trip to Jerusalem.

Sadat visited the Yad Vashem Holocaust memorial for the six million Jews killed by the Nazis, as was customary for presidents and heads of government. It was a must for them – to see Israel's "raison d'etre." Sadat was deeply moved. During the tour of the memorial, an Egyptian journalist said: "What gruesome pictures of Jews killed by the Nazis. I cannot express what I feel. But I begin to understand the mentality of the Israelis."

Anwar Sadat speaking in the Knesset, November 1977

To Cairo

I was one of the first foreign correspondents to travel to Cairo after Sadat visited Israel. I figured that if Sadat could come to Jerusalem, I could go to Cairo. I showed up in the city on December 26, 1977, a little more than a month after Sadat had visited Jerusalem. My preparations were meticulous. Nothing should reveal that I came from Israel, at that time still a hostile country in the eyes of many Egyptians. They did not know yet of the new and more pleasant wind blowing from the pyramids. So, I removed all labels of Israeli dry-cleaning firms from my clothes and made sure that even my toothpaste would not give me away.

I was in close touch with the Danish foreign ministry regarding how I should go. "Travel via the Danish embassy in Cyprus," they said. "We will arrange a new passport for you there."

I showed up in the Danish diplomatic mission in Nicosia and obtained a brand new passport. There were a lot of Egyptians on the plane to Cairo. We did not talk much. The less, the better. Then somebody announced that an American journalist had just been shot in Cairo. We were shocked. "Too late to return," I said to myself. "Make the best of it."

We landed at Cairo Airport. Nobody questioned why I had a brand new passport. So far, so good. I was met by a Swedish UN officer I knew from Jerusalem. He had arranged hotel accommodation for me. When he drove me to the hotel I noticed it was way out of town, so I told him that I wanted to be in downtown Cairo, in the hub. Somehow through the Scandinavian grapevine he managed to get me a room at a quaint family-type hotel, Horus House, on Zamalek Island, in the middle of the city.

There I made my headquarters for the next few days. The foreign editor of my paper at the time, *Jyllands-Posten*, had arranged for comprehensive coverage of the new situation by sending a journalist also to Tripoli to report simultaneously from another part of the Arab world.

Zamalek is a delightful place, with shops and an atmosphere reminding one of Paris. I was all alone and felt it. Fortunately, however, in the

112

solitude of my hotel room I managed to find a broadcast from Tel Aviv with happy songs.

All over, loudspeakers blared Sadat's speech at the Knesset. But it would soon be clear that the population as such did not know about the new tides.

I rented a taxi with a guide driver, who said that he would be with me all day and wait for me at my various stops. First I decided to go to Cairo University and interview students. Sporting various cameras, I arrived at the entrance to the institution – the press at work. At the entrance stood two mighty gorillas as guardsmen. Somehow I managed to get by them and soon found myself surrounded by students who wanted to have contact with a foreign journalist.

Among the students were two sisters who were studying nothing other than Hebrew at the university. We had a good conversation about Sadat showing the way. Then the two gorillas showed up at my shoulders, inquiring who I was and what I was doing.

A mild arrest in Cairo

"You are under arrest," they said, shoving me to a room in the administration building. "The president wants to see you," they told me. "But first we must take your passport."

I said, glancing at my watch: "You may have my passport for twenty minutes, no more, because I have an important appointment and I am never late for meetings."

I sat down and waited. I had tried to show them I would not give up easily. After twenty minutes the gorillas came back and said: "Cairo University's president salutes you and says you are welcome to come back and interview students anytime."

"I also salute him," I responded. "I may come back."

I got into my taxi. The driver told me that he had been worried stiff about me. I hired him on the spot to take me to an entertainment area in Sahara City, not far from the pyramids, that evening.

I sat by myself in the restaurant and tried to find out what was going on. The guests were contributing money to Sadat's peace initiative. Most of the money came from rich Saudi people. The amounts and the names of the givers were announced. I contributed a hundred Egyptian pounds, not a small amount. "Who is the giver?" the master of ceremonies inquired. I told him my name. "And where are you from?" he wanted to know. "Jerusalem," I said. The guests in the restaurant turned their heads to see the creature. Then one clapped his hands, and the others followed suit.

During the next few days I got to know many Egyptians. I found that they were a very friendly people who had been exploited by other Arab countries and were now looking inward to find their rightful place as the leader of the Arab world. I was at a journalists' party one evening and could not find a taxi to take me to my hotel. Then I decided to walk, quite a long way. People I stopped on my way to ask directions were quite helpful. I felt at home.

The cacophony from the traffic was something new. The sound of donkeys, camels and car horns was overwhelming. Already then Cairo was the undisputed center in the Arab world. Its name Kahira, meaning the victorious or triumphant, is actually taken from the planet Mars (El Kahir). I have since been many times to this great city, always staying at Horus House. Several of these visits were organized by the Government

Press Office in Jerusalem, whose director took three of his smartest secretaries with him to help us have a smooth visit.

I had another interesting experience in Cairo. All the countries who had declared Sadat an enemy for his peace initiative with Israel wanted to show their refusal of his politics by breaking off diplomatic relations with Egypt. They did it in a very special way.

I watched much of it from my observation post in Zamalek. Vanloads of office furniture and other equipment left the embassies of these rejectionist countries – and after circling the building, the trucks unloaded their cargo at a side entrance. A veritable circus. So much for breaking diplomatic relations.

Arrested in Egypt

On one of my trips to Jordan I decided to return in a rather unorthodox way, by ship from Aqaba to Nuweiba in Egypt, some sixty miles south of Eilat. I wanted to go by sea to enjoy a new experience.

I had a fellow traveler, a Swiss journalist by the name of Jacques (I shall not reveal his last name) based in Jerusalem, and he was also interested in the voyage. We boarded the ship together with several hundred Palestinian workers, who had been in Saudi Arabia and were on their way home.

We got acquainted with the captain, a staunch sailor, and he invited us up on the bridge for – as he put it – "a Middle East talk." He told us that he was very impressed by the Israeli historian Benny Morris, who had changed his position and now revealed that Israeli troops had killed many Palestinians fleeing the newly declared state of Israel. "Morris is a courageous man," the captain said. "If there were more like him, peace might come."

About thirty miles from Nuweiba, a man from the Egyptian passport police appeared and demanded to see our passports. He put them in his pocket. We wanted them back but he refused, saying we would get them in Egypt. We insisted on getting them back there and then, but he declined. Even when we told him that this situation might lead to a diplomatic incident with Switzerland and Denmark he did not budge.

We got to Nuweiba, a desert resort, and took our luggage the long way to an administration building, where – we were told – we would get our passports back. The passport official who had taken our documents was nowhere to be seen. We were locked up in a room and told we were under arrest until the matter was clarified.

Jacques was devastated. He got very tense, not least by looking out of a window and seeing lots of Egyptians soldiers exercising. I tried to calm him down. "Now you must show them who is the effendi [the man in command]," I said. I got up and audaciously opened a desk drawer. There were dozens of passports. I dug down and found ours. Then I announced to the guard outside that we were leaving. He was speechless. Upon exiting the building, I spotted a taxi stand nearby. "Let's take a taxi to Eilat," I suggested to Jacques. And so we did.

On another one of my visits to Egypt I witnessed Sadat and Begin dividing the Middle East between them, as if it were the meeting of Churchill, Stalin and Roosevelt in Yalta, where they divided the world up into spheres of interest at the end of World War II. From a hotel lobby on Elephantine Island in 1980, we journalists could see the two state leaders sitting on the edge of a swimming pool, with a big map spread out in front of them. It was like seeing world history enacted in front of us – these two powerful men engaging in a give-and-take of the Middle East.

I remember a talk I had with Sadat's daughter, Jihan, who worked as a secretary for her father at the time. She exuded happiness that day. "I'm so happy because today I got divorced," this twenty-two-year-old beauty said to me. "I have been married to a rascal and only found out late."

President Sadat and Prime Minister Begin at a hotel swimming pool on Elephantine Island, Egypt, in 1980, dividing the Middle East between them.

Dialogue with Egyptians

I visited Egypt several times after Hosni Mubarak took over as president following the assassination of Anwar Sadat.

The Egyptians, I learned, were quite happy about the peaceful relations with Israel; they did not want to fight other Arab countries' wars against Israel. I also discovered that a dialogue with an Egyptian could be very fictitious.

Sitting across from an Egyptian in a Cairo café, we both spoke English. So we thought. But the other party did not quite understand what was said. We talked past one another. He did not understand what I said, but he was polite, smiled and nodded his head. So did I when he spoke, out of courtesy. We parted in a friendly atmosphere, still not understanding what each other had meant.

What I did understand from other conversations was that the Egyptians missed Sadat and paid tribute to him for what he had done for peace, and that they hoped Mubarak would be an equally good man for Egypt by raising the standard of living.

In the middle of April 1982, I visited Cairo again to gauge the atmosphere before Egypt was to take over the last part of the Sinai, from which Israel was withdrawing, and to get an idea of whether Mubarak's Egypt was different from that of Sadat's. I found that the Egyptians were not taken up by the fact that soon they would get their lost land back. Israel's withdrawal was not the hot topic that one would have expected. What one talked about in Cairo was the price of pita bread, football, a scandal about imported rotten food, a resumption of diplomatic relations with countries in the Arab world, the lack of onions so important to the Egyptian diet and the shortfall of engineers.

The economy was Egypt's most serious problem. According to Mubarak, the economy was headed for catastrophe unless the alarming population increase was halted. At that time Egypt had forty-four million inhabitants – as of 2014 it has eighty-six million – with an increase of over one million annually at the time.

The "p-pill" was produced locally, but only few used it. The reason for families with many children – a well-informed Egyptian told me – was that women wanted to give birth to a "suitable" amount of children in order to prove to other women that they were still young. I was even told that some women would sell their pills as food for cattle instead of using them. Men also liked to have many children, hoping that the children would support the father when he got old, as per the classic family pattern.

Even though the absence of Sadat was still greatly felt, it was clear that he was belittled in Egypt at the time because he liked too much to be in the international limelight. He had been fond of being seen with the world's greatest and he had been a flamboyant "showman," too extravagant in his dress, a spendthrift with residences all over Egypt. The worst one might say about Sadat was that he did not deal with the Egyptian society's basic problems – support of state-owned industry, subsidies to essential foods, the acute lack of housing and the import policy.

Mubarak, on the other hand, was another type with a more sober style. He knew what bothered the ordinary Egyptian and tried to do something about it. His lifestyle was more modest and more realistic than that of Sadat. One of the first things he did after coming to power was to give up the many residences at the president's disposal in various parts of the country. He focused on Egypt's most painful problem, the economy, and encouraged increased investment in industry and established subsidies for the lowest salaried. One of his goals was to prevent the gap between rich and poor from growing.

The most important thing to Mubarak was that his rule should be efficient. It started with his appearance in his office at 8:00 a.m., earlier than is usual for an Egyptian head of state. At that hour Mubarak would call his associates to find out what they were doing. To begin with, not many ministers began work so early, but they soon lived up to the new style. A Western ambassador I talked with in Cairo said that one could clearly see the new style and spirit in government offices. The offices were kept clean and tidy – in other words, efficiency was the name of the game.

However, poverty in Cairo was as widespread as ever, with families squatting in the entrances of new apartment houses. To the observer, Mubarak's policies were misdirected. Typical of the economy then was that a government official would earn some 80 Egyptian pounds (about $100) per month and a police officer much less. A three-room apartment would cost 30 pounds in rent monthly. Because of rent control, a European embassy would pay 60 pounds in rent for a very large apartment in the fashionable Zamalek neighborhood – while the same embassy would pay 1,600 pounds monthly for a far smaller apartment for its first secretary.

Mubarak admonished that the Israeli withdrawal from Sinai did not mean that the Egyptians "would find gold there," but more work and sweat "for our paralyzing economic problems," as he put it. On the plus side, Egypt had just opened a car tunnel under the Suez Canal connecting Africa and Asia. The tunnel, which also has a fresh water conduit carrying water from the Nile to Sinai, announced the Egyptian development projects for the desert peninsula. Cairo – I was told – planned to settle many Egyptians in Sinai and exploit the area's resources, comprising oil and minerals. Two more tunnels were planned nearby.

What one did not discuss, but what the Israelis were keenly aware of, was that the tunnels could be used to transport a large Egyptian army quickly through Sinai toward Israel.

The "Real" Hebrews

Since 1969 a group of some twenty-two hundred African Americans have lived in the south of Israel, claiming that they are the "real" Hebrews and that the whites have usurped the country.

They claim to be the descendants of the lost tribes of Israel. They are called "the black Hebrews" and live in Dimona, Arad, Mitzpe Ramon and other cities in the south, and in an area near Tiberius in the Galilee. An official at the American embassy in Tel Aviv says "they are a sect, not a cult." They say that they are Israel's true heirs, that others have taken the land from them but that they are now settling in.

The Black Hebrews in Dimona, 1978

The Israelis originally tended to view this group with skepticism. There were numerous scandals, including complaints from residents of Dimona and allegations that children in the group were beaten. Moreover, an ax murder took place during a feud between rivaling factions in the group. But in the late 1970s there were fewer scandals. The conduct of the black Hebrews became almost exemplary – no crimes, no drugs. They improved their reputation so that their status in the country was changed from tourists to temporary residents.

"But the black Hebrews have not become Israeli citizens, and they neither do military service nor pay taxes," said a Ministry of Interior spokesman. "They have, however, received Israeli identity cards."

When the African Americans began entering Israel as tourists in 1969, their leaders stated that they were the forerunners of two to three million Americans who intended to come here. They said that it was "their country" and that the white Jews in Israel are imposters, because it is the black people who are the true Hebrews of the Bible.

At the time, Israeli experts said that the black people in the United States had devised a plan to go to Israel, claiming to be Jews, in order to secure a new existence for themselves as free people without any discrimination. The majority of them were born in Chicago and came to Israel after a stay in Liberia, where many of them lived with extended families.

Their leader for many years, Ben Ami Ben-Israel, originally Ben Carter, left Chicago some forty years ago with 430 of his followers and took them deep into Liberia's jungle. They lived there for two years under difficult conditions, in inadequate tents and suffering from dysentery, until he brought them to Israel. He says that he, like Moses, was chosen to set his people free from suffering and bring them to the Promised Land. His followers call him the Messiah.

Of his original 430 in Liberia, 75 percent returned to the United States. The black Hebrews came to Israel almost unnoticed, but their number increased from 120 to 300 in 1971. Now there are more than eight times as many of them.

The Israeli authorities were perplexed about how to deal with the African Americans. They would have preferred not to have anything to do with them, because they feared that the approximately forty million blacks in the United States, who thought that Israel could offer them a better existence, would pour into the country in large numbers.

Besides this concern, the initial influx began positively. The Israelis were unprepared for the arrivals, and must have expected the types of black Jews from the United States that they were familiar with, such as the entertainer Sammy Davis Jr. However, the situation took a negative turn. Some of the last black Americans to arrive were not interested in working, but formed music groups that resulted in unrest in the neighborhood.

Others caused an "incident," when thirty of them helped themselves to supplies at a supermarket without paying, but only after having made sure that the foreign TV and press would be there to witness the scene. Their stay in Israel began like a "love affair," but developed into a bitter situation accompanied by threats that the blacks would take over Israel as their "biblical right."

The African Americans live in their own world, both physically and mentally. In Dimona – where I visited them – most of them live in their group's own district, a former immigration center in the outskirts of the city. Here, they have started an unusual religious movement and established a peculiar social order. They have their own system of government and education.

"We were originally sixteen black families who left the United States for Liberia and from there for Israel," says one of the black Hebrews, whose name I do not remember. He told me the following fascinating story of how the group perceives its background and claim to Israel.

"We are the descendants of the Children of Israel," he said. "There were twelve tribes. The Jews stem from the tribe of Judah, but we do not. We have been asked, several times, to convert to Judaism, first and foremost by national-religious people, but we have rejected such a proposal. Our forefathers were once in Assyrian imprisonment, and as a result of the weakness of biblical Israel, we were sent into captivity again – to Egypt where we remained throughout 430 years. From there our ancestors went to Sudan, then southward in Africa, and at last to the west coast of Africa, where the Arabs enslaved us again and sent us to the United States and into renewed bondage."

He continued his story of the group's dramatic history: "In a broad sense the United States became a place of slavery for us, much like Egypt was for our forefathers. White Americans pushed us into black ghettos and told us that we were 'wild' and that we used to run around half naked in the jungle with bows and arrows.

"We knew that David and Solomon were our forefathers, but the American authorities took the Old Testament away from us. They gave us the New Testament and said that Jesus had brought everything to fulfillment and that we, therefore, no longer needed the Old Testament.

It was a kind of religious conspiracy to keep us down. We know that we have now returned. We did not return on our own. God has done it. We are in His kingdom."

"How are you organized?" I asked the former farmer from Georgia.

"We have established a new world order," he said. "God's kingdom is a sign to all that one can begin to live anew. We are organized in a divine fashion that pleases God. Religiously we live like Moses. Our lives are based on the Ten Commandments."

I spoke next with the group's spokeswoman. Born in Chicago, this fifty-three-year-old woman had changed her name from Freda Waller to Jaffa Bat Israel. Jaffa told me about the black Hebrew's system of government: "Ben-Ami is our spiritual leader. His immediate subordinates are twelve princes, who are not elected, but installed in their office. Below the princes are twelve ministers, and under them are thirty-five so-called *arturim* consisting of twenty-five women and ten men. All these leaders take care of our daily activities and some of them are contacts to the municipality of Dimona."

Jaffa, who originally studied medicine at the Catholic Loyola University in Chicago, came to Israel in 1976 at the age of eighteen. She had heard about the black Hebrew's existence from an older sister, who was a member of this society. Her parents are still in the United States. She was married for seven years. Her ex-husband, Elkareem Ben Israel, is a basketball trainer in northern Israel.

"Our lives are good in Israel," she said. "We feel that we live right with our hearts, souls and bodies. We share in the economy and our human resources. We have created a society that for us is Utopia."

"We are somewhat frustrated that we are not fully integrated into the Israeli society, but we have seen some progress," she said "We are overjoyed that Ben Ami had the wisdom to see that the time was right to leave the United States and return to our homeland. We were the victims of the slave trade from Africa to North America in the 1500s. We are part of the tribes of Israel – also called "Israel's children" or the Hebrew Israelites. We have a tradition that among other things includes a woman's purity during her menstrual period (Leviticus 15:19–24). My grandmother held on to this tradition, going to ritual baths, which corresponded to the Jewish mikvah. We have no synagogue, but we strictly observe the day of rest, the Sabbath, by not doing any form of work, nor driving a car."

Dimona's vice-mayor, Gadi Lanuch, told me that the city's government, together with the leaders of the black Hebrews, have had many meetings with representatives of the Israeli public administration, the Foreign Affairs and the Internal Affairs ministries, and that many offers have been put forward from the Israeli side about improvements in the conditions for the black Hebrews, but without any results.

"We look upon the black Hebrews as a positive element in the city, and they are well integrated into our society," Lanuch told me. "The biggest problem now is the lack of housing. They live in small apartments with too many people crowded together. There is another problem, too. The black Hebrews do not waste time in dealing with thieves, drug addicts and prostitutes. They simply throw them out. But this does not solve the problem, because they still remain within Israel's borders."

The black Hebrews' way of life is quite unique. They live according to their own special rules of conduct. Polygamy is permitted and birth control is forbidden. Their leaders decree who will marry whom, performing the weddings and approving annulments. They are vegetarians, do not drink alcohol and do not smoke. They are against homosexuality, and premarital sexual activity is not allowed. Young people are always accompanied by older chaperones, and the society teaches them to be abstinent before marriage. The marriageable age has gone up. Twenty years ago, sixteen and seventeen year olds were getting married, now they are twenty-one and twenty-two year olds.

They are a very colorful community. They wear multicolored clothes made of natural materials such as cotton, wool or silk (Leviticus 19:19). The men wear crocheted skullcaps, mostly white, and the women white kerchiefs. They describe the way they dress as a mixture of their forefathers dress with an "Eastern" flavor.

They do not wear leather shoes, because leather derives from animals that have been killed. Instead they wear crocheted shoes. The women wear long dresses. All boys are circumcised when they are eight days old (Genesis 17:9–14).

"We have no burglaries, and we never lock our doors," Jaffa said.

The black Hebrews earn their livelihood as unskilled construction workers, by producing health food in their own factory, or as performing musicians in Israel. The group's observance of the Bible is in certain aspects stricter than in other religions. Every Sabbath is a fast day in order to rest the body as much as possible. As Ben Ami told me, "The Sabbath is a day of complete rest and fasting. It's almost as though we have fifty-two Yom Kippur holidays a year."

The group enforces strict discipline – the children bow when they greet adults and wives submit completely to their husbands. Some people perceive their discipline as cultish behavior, but the black Hebrews think of it as a necessary antidote against the collapse of the American black family unit and against the black street culture that they do not approve of.

As to their relationship to Dimona's other citizens, Jaffa said that they have come to have mutual respect for each other. "In the beginning they called us Negroes, but that is no longer done," she said.

The life the black Hebrews live is so attractive for some that several non-blacks have sought to become members of the society. "We accept white people, provided that they adopt our lifestyle," Jaffa said. "We do not accept anyone who drinks or smokes. Two white women and two white men live in our society today. All four are single.

"Our biggest problem is lack of housing," she continued. "An apartment with four rooms may house thirty people. Married couples have their own rooms, but the children sleep together. All rooms are filled with mattresses. At least eight hundred children have been born to the black Hebrews since 1970. Over six hundred children aged three to sixteen years have their meals in a large dining hall in ten shifts. A kitchen staff of six women work here from 4:00 a.m. until 10:00 p.m., under the leadership of the kitchen chef, Nehamayah."

The group's founder and leader, Ben Ami Ben-Israel, was born in Chicago. He is a former metallurgist and was the wrestling champion of Illinois in the beginning of the 1960s. He is a stately man dressed in a colorful tunic with ornamentations. In his hand is a wooden scepter, just like an African chieftain.

About the acceptance of the group by the Ministry of Internal Affairs, he said: "It is like a dream that has become reality. Israel has now accepted its responsibility for its sons, who have come home from exile in North America. I thank God for having experienced this day."

Ben Ami rejected Israel's fear that the group has a hidden agenda and was secretly preparing for the immigration of many millions of blacks from Africa and North America. According to him there are at most a few thousand black Hebrew Jews abroad – in the United States, England and West Africa – who wish to come to Israel. "They are the descendants of the biblical Israelites, and they would not come to Israel for materialistic, but for spiritual reasons," he said.

There have been sporadic attempts in Israel to deport the black Hebrews. The government of Israel has avoided this, but at the same time also refrained from granting the black Hebrews citizenship or permanent residency. The attempts of deportation were unsuccessful because the group had collectively renounced their American citizenship. Since they were stateless, Israel could not deport them for lack of a place to send them to. In 1986, according to Jaffa, Israel deported forty-six men, aged seventeen to sixty, because they worked without a work permit. However, this deportation was an exception.

Ben Ami told me that the black Hebrews regard themselves as Jews as far as their tribal origin is concerned, but that their nationality is Israelite – "Hebrew Israelites, descendants of Abraham and Jacob."

It is a slow process to obtain Israeli citizenship, but it is bound to happen eventually. There are third-generation children here who are stateless, because their parents did not remain in the United States long enough for them to automatically become American citizens. In spite of their difficulty with Israeli authorities, the black Hebrews say that their lives in Dimona are far better than they would have been in the United States.

"We have created a society here, where we, with exceptional devotion, live a pure and strictly disciplined life," said the above-mentioned farmer from Georgia.

Melodi Grand Prix Winner – Three Times

In April 1978, Israel won the Melodi Grand Prix song contest, accompanied by blaring car horns and singing in the streets by overwhelmed Israelis. The winner was the Israeli song group Alpha Beta, whose star was Izhar Cohen, aged twenty-seven, with his catchy song "A-ba-ni-bi" – a sort of children's code language for "I love you."

The song contest was held in Paris. Throughout the night, well-wishers streamed to his parents' home in the Tel Aviv suburb of Givatayim. Izhar Cohen has a Yemenite background. When we met in Tel Aviv he told me that not only was the prize a show of support to Israel at a time when Israel felt isolated, it was also a recognition of the Oriental (Mizrachi) part of Israel's population, which considered itself to be unfairly treated compared to the inhabitants of European extraction.

An average of eight votes from nineteen European countries was a great boost to the Israelis, who felt that the world had discovered their country. "We see it is an extra plus that the song was in Hebrew, a language that only a few people in the world understand," Izhar told me.

In March 1979, Israel – as the winner – hosted the Eurovision song contest. It was held at the International Convention Center Binyanei Ha'uma, near the Hilton Hotel, today named the Crowne Plaza. Security for the event was enormous, to the extent that the press covering it had to stay at the hotel for several days, before and after the song contest. No business as usual. Hundreds of people of the press from all over had to settle down in that hotel until the winner was declared.

Tension was high. Israel won for the second year in a row, and the Israelis were ecstatic. The winner was Gali Atari with her hit song "Hallelujah," performed by the group Milk and Honey. It was a popular choice. A resounding success. For the press it was the end of several days of imprisonment.

Again, it was a tribute to the Yemenite culture in Israel. Gali Atari, like Izhar Cohen before her, is of Yemenite background, and their community in Israel felt that her victory was a boost to their morale.

Gali later told me that "Hallelujah" CDs were sold by the millions, even more than Abba's "Waterloo." I met with Gali – a gazelle-like, charming twenty-six year old – in a music studio in Tel Aviv, where Milk and Honey worked seven hours a day. She told me that "Hallelujah" had already been translated into Danish, Swedish, Norwegian, Samish, Portuguese, Spanish, Italian, Greek and Japanese.

She also told me that she believed her group would become a world success. Her career as a singer had begun in 1975 when she, together with an Israeli musical group, performed on Broadway in New York with a musical. She demonstrated her versatility then by succeeding as a movie actress at a high level.

Dana International, third Israeli winner of the Eurovision

To date, Israel has won the contest three times. The third time was in 1998, almost twenty years after "Hallelujah," when the Israeli singer Dana International in Birmingham took top honors with the song "Diva," setting off widespread celebrations in Israel.

There was much focus on Dana because of her achievement, but also because of her sex change. She began life as a man by the name of Yaron Cohen, but in 1994 underwent a sex-change operation in London – and came out of the closet. Now she could perform as the woman she had wanted to be from the time of her early youth.

I met Dana in a music studio in Tel Aviv and found a flamboyant personality. She sings disco songs with a Madonna-like fervor. She has a pretty, warm voice, charm and natural charisma.

"Her participation as Israel's official representative shows that Israel is a modern, liberal society, and her victory made us happy and proud," one Israeli said. Another Israeli had just the opposite opinion. "It is a big embarrassment to Israel that this happened," he said, and refused to talk about the Israeli singer as a woman. He stressed that he will always refer to her as a man.

Dana also is yet another Israeli singer of Yemenite descent. When I discussed this with her, she commented: "There may be an Oriental attraction to our song. It is not only a victory for me as a person, but for Israel and its image."

The news of Dana's victory was received in Israel with mixed feelings. She told me that she was very happy that Israel officially let her represent the country at an international event. "It is high time that a transsexual person receives such recognition by his or her country," she said. "I am proud that Israel chose me. I am happy to show that there are other sides of Israel than scenes of violence. My parents are even happier than I am. Now they say that they can hold their heads high for the rest of their lives."

Arabic youth in Israel paid tribute to Dana as a singer and as an expression of progress. A twenty-five-year-old Arabic woman, Abir Sa'adi of East Jerusalem, said: "Dana is a sign of the times and it was absolutely important that she won. She represents what goes on today. We live at a time when there is ambiguity between the sexes. We are in a new phase now. Dana won because of her song and performance, but I am convinced that her personal story also contributed to her victory. She is very courageous in her music and lyrics about different kinds of women. She has accomplished something great. She is simply brilliant."

Because of Israel's participation in the Eurovision Song Contest, many Arab states that were eligible to participate decided not to do so. Tunisia, Morocco and Lebanon are cases in point.

Kollek the Charismatic

His first name was Theodor. But everybody called him Teddy.

Teddy Kollek was Jerusalem's legendary and charismatic mayor from 1965, when he was fifty-four years old, and for twenty-eight years onward until he was eighty-two. His imprint on Jerusalem was unique. Not since biblical times has so much been done for the city by one man.

Two years after he became the mayor of West Jerusalem, his domain was extended to include East Jerusalem, after the two parts were united under Israel. I knew him quite well. I could go and see him in his office almost anytime. Years before we had traveled together to Denmark for his unveiling of a large Israeli stone placed on "Israel Square" in downtown Copenhagen. We exchanged a lot of banter. Ever since then he liked to greet me with "What's new in the Kingdom of Denmark?"

Born in Vienna, he came to Palestine in 1935, where he became a founding member of Kibbutz Ein Gev, on the shores of Lake Tiberias. During World War II he was the contact man to the Jewish underground movement in Israel. After Israel's independence was declared, he went into government service.

He was reelected five times. Even the Arabs in East Jerusalem voted for him, and he won by a large majority over all challengers, until he was felled by a rightist–ultra-Orthodox coalition. He was so popular that he even got votes from the Likud rightwing party, who switched to voting for Kollek because of his personality.

One of my several interviews with Teddy Kollek took place in 1984, when he was seventy-three years old and could look forward to another full-time position for four and a half years. Jerusalem's super-mayor seemed to be quite unaffected by his age. "It is a long time until my period as a mayor expires," he said. "It is too early to talk about whether I will continue afterwards."

Kollek told me that he was not interested in anniversaries, but admitted that he was nevertheless planning to mark three big ones:

131

1) December 1, 1985 – the twentieth anniversary of his becoming mayor, 2) May 27, 1987 – his seventy-fifth birthday and 3) June 1987 – twenty years after the reunification of Jerusalem. "I would like to use all these dates to get money for Jerusalem," he said.

Kollek and myself

Teddy Kollek was Israel's greatest fund-raiser. Many well-to-do people all over the world wanted to be with him – but that always cost them a pretty penny. He enlisted renowned city planners and architects to help plan how Jerusalem should look. He had supporters among the world's important Jews, as well as non-Jews. He skirted getting money from the Jerusalem municipality "because it was stingy" and instead established the "Jerusalem Foundation," an organization through which he could conduct fund-raising without disclosing the source.

Through the foundation, Jerusalem experienced a wealth of creativity unknown in its long history – parks, museums and a music center were established. Above all, Kollek is known as the founder of the great

Israel Museum, and his memory will live long into the future thanks to Jerusalem's large football stadium, which was named for him.

During the interview, Kollek told me that he was out checking the streets of the city already at 6:00 a.m., to see which were in order and which needed attention. He said that Jerusalem was a poor city, with relatively little industry, no major enterprises, and with 80 percent of its more than half a million inhabitants being first- and second-generation immigrants – Jews as well as Arabs. Many of them were drawn to Jerusalem because it was the holy city, and they would spend their last years there.

It was Jerusalem's and perhaps also the Middle East's good luck that Kollek was its mayor during the critical periods during and after the Six-day War. He had the vision and ability to make the two halves of the city function as one unit.

A man of many talents, Kollek was a cheered master of ceremonies at jazz concerts, he got the ball rolling at major football matches and he was quick witted. He was once asked whether he would prefer to be the mayor of New York or San Francisco. "For New York I'm not witty enough, and for San Francisco I'm not pretty enough," was his answer. He invented the "Teddy talk" – he would appear briefly at an event to say a few words, and then make a fast escape.

I asked him what he thought of a possible Jordanian presence in Jerusalem, perhaps with a Jordanian flag. He answered: "I can accept a religious Arabic flag or another flag flying above the mosques – but not above the Temple Mount. I can imagine that the Saudis will say that they are the guardians of the holy places and that their flag should be there. I would not object to such flags over the mosques of Jerusalem. For me it is the same as having the Israeli flag over the synagogue on Fifth Avenue in New York. We are all too suspicious and narrow-minded. But Jerusalem must never be divided. Today this city has greater freedom for religion and church service, respect for the holy places and freedom of the press than it had under the Turks, British and Jordanians."

Asked about the Arab population in Jerusalem, Kollek said: "It is unpleasant to belong to a minority, especially one facing the possibility of more wars and with relatives in Arab countries. But this does not change the fact that the Arabs in Jerusalem have equality before the law. It will take some years until they receive the same service, but we have taken several important steps in that direction."

Another question was to what extent the Arabs in Jerusalem supported him, to which he answered: "In the eyes of the Arabs, I am a lesser evil. I have obtained a close personal relationship with many Arabs, who admit that more is being done for them now than earlier. I try to help them with education and medical assistance, and I intervene if, for example, a road is being built too close to an Arab village in the outskirts of Jerusalem. This naturally gives me friends among the Arabs."

One of Kollek's close associates, Avraham Avi-hai, has revealed new sides of Kollek in a recent article in an Israeli newspaper. "Teddy was not a pushover," he wrote. "He had a temper and with age it became more and more pronounced. With age, fame and perhaps too many yes-men, Teddy played the curmudgeon. 'Don't talk to me unless you have a check.' In most cases he got the check.

"At an Israel Museum board meeting, Teddy appeared wearing a tie, a gift from a well-meaning donor. Teddy began his welcome address: 'You all see I own a tie. Now that you've seen it, I can take it off.'"

Avi-hai also wrote about how Teddy became the mayor. He had resigned from the prime minister's office. Kollek was an avowed Ben-Gurionist, who could no longer bridge the vast chasm separating Ben-Gurion and his successor, Levi Eshkol. "Photographer David Rubinger and I lamented Israel's loss of Teddy's immense talents," Avi-hai wrote. "How could Teddy only run a private business when the country needed his powerful leadership and ability?" Then Rubinger and Avi-hai had a brainstorm: "How about Teddy becoming the mayor of Jerusalem?"

They both thought of the same upcoming event to launch their idea: a concert by the philharmonic at the Jerusalem International Convention Center, Binyanei Ha'uma. Everybody who counted would be there. They decided to start a rumor. They went around whispering into people's ears, as if it were a secret: "Did you hear that Teddy is running for mayor of Jerusalem?" Their tactic paid off. When Teddy was told of it many years later, he was totally surprised.

The Hotel That Woke Up
in Another Country

A few miles south of Israel's vacation paradise Eilat is a ten-story, five-star luxury hotel, which on one November day in 1982 woke up in a different country from where it was built. Hotel Avia Sonesta, as it was called, was and is a great attraction, and its leadership termed it the most spectacular in the Middle East at the time.

It was slated for opening on November 15, in the presence of four hundred specially invited guests. A press conference, to which I was invited, was scheduled to take place earlier that same day. But that was not for me; I wanted to have my story already in the Scandinavian papers on opening day. My visit a week earlier was okayed by the hotel's PR department. I felt tension in the air at my arrival. Here was a great edifice, soon to change nationality – if a building can do so.

The hotel is located in the Taba Bay and was one of fifteen border points on which Egypt and Israel had not agreed when Israel withdrew from Sinai six months earlier. The old borderline, dating from Israel's establishment in 1948, was an armistice demarcation line. The Israelis maintained that the international border was actually somewhat to the south, in Wadi Taba. Israel argued this with maps, drawn up by the British in 1906. If Israel was right, the hotel was on Israeli territory. But the Egyptians said that by opening the hotel, Israel had annexed the area de facto.

In order to decide on the fifteen unresolved border points, the Egyptian foreign minister Mohammed Hassan Ali and the Israeli defense minister Ariel Sharon had flown over the disputed area and agreed on a solution to all the problems – except the Taba Bay. They decided that everything should continue as before in Taba, and the Israelis interpreted this to mean that they could complete building the hotel – and open it.

I wanted to take a picture of the hotel from above to show how it was situated and decided to climb a nearby hill – a rather dangerous undertaking, which I could not begin without first getting permission from the Israeli military authorities in Tel Aviv. This was granted, and a young officer was assigned as my escort.

We began our climb upward, rocks and stones rolling down wherever we set our feet. The scenery was breathtaking. Down below was the blue Red Sea, in the distance somewhat to the south was Saudi Arabia and nearby was Jordan.

We passed an Israeli military post. "Careful," they said. "We will keep an eye on you and help if you need it." Further up we came to a plateau with a border pole. I took pictures in all directions. There was a lot of birdlife and even gazelles up there. I felt like we were about to enter paradise. It was incredibly beautiful. Down below we could see the hotel and next to us border pole no. 91.

The picture I took of Hotel Avia Sonesta from a height of several hundred feet. (Note border pole 91 in the foreground.)

Climbing down a steep hill is usually more difficult than climbing up. We went down like skiers, with feet parallel to one another in order not to lose our balance and fall. More stones and rocks flew down. It took us double the time to descend.

I had my pictures developed fast and realized that I had some quite extraordinary photos, which were presumably unique. A newspaper in Tel Aviv bought the right to use them and I sent them by special delivery to the paper. It was published the following day. *Time* magazine also bought the right to the pictures – but never used them.

The hotel was termed an architectural masterpiece, built by architect Uri Blumenthal of Tel Aviv. It had all the facilities. The swimming pool was shaped as a large flower, with a circular bar-island in the middle. It had its own beach for sports diving and sailing and five tennis courts with an adjoining tennis "clinic," according to the American concept. It boasted 340 rooms, ten suites, five restaurants and a ballroom with space for five hundred guests.

A gem in the desert.

Car Equilibrist in Lebanon

Israel went to war against the PLO in Lebanon on June 6, 1982 – not against Lebanon, but against the Palestinian guerillas who were attacking goals in Israel from within Lebanon. Already in April of that year it was rumored that Israel would attack the PLO north of the border in revenge for the murder of an Israeli diplomat in Paris. "We never talk about troop movements," an Israeli military spokesman said to me on April 12.

Two months later Israel struck across the border, in an attempt to eliminate the PLO forces. The Israeli military movement was swift. The PLO was quickly defeated and hundreds of PLO men taken prisoner. I went up north with the Israeli army, passing Palestinian refugee camps along the way. In many places Lebanese citizens stood at the roadside and greeted the Israeli troops with flowers because they had gotten rid of the PLO.

Soon after crossing the border at Rosh HaNikra I realized that my journey would be even more adventurous than expected. The road was wide, sometimes with six lanes, and it soon developed into a strange thoroughfare in which every second lane was headed in an alternate direction. What a mess, I said to myself. It was utterly dangerous. One had to be a car equilibrist to make the journey.

I eventually arrived in Beirut, a war-ravaged city that had been partially taken by the Israeli army. There, standing on the top floor of a high-rise building, I witnessed Israeli soldiers firing through blown-out windows at PLO fighters in a house a few hundred yards away.

For the families of Israeli soldiers, the war was terribly difficult. The Israeli army has a rule that members of the same family may not fight on the same front for fear that a brother might kill his sibling in "friendly fire," but the army was not strict about maintaining this principle. It was a nightmare for the families.

A journalist colleague of mine, father of an Israeli soldier, told me that he was constantly writing articles for his newspaper in order not to think about his son in battle. He tried not to imagine that any minute, the doorbell would ring and two officers standing outside would tell him that his son had been killed.

One young Israeli soldier told me that he had been in one of three armored personnel carriers (APCs) moving along in the Lake Qaraoun area, when a Syrian fighter plane opened fire on the Israeli convoy. The first APC exploded, sending the men skyward. The second vehicle caught fire. Nothing happened to the third APC, but its commander had the gruesome task of ordering his men out with plastic bags to gather the limbs of dead fellow soldiers with whom they had talked just minutes earlier. This incident burned itself deep into the minds of the soldiers in the third APC. Some of them to this day relive those awful moments – a psychological price of the war.

With steel helmet, Lebanon, 1982

My attire during war trips in Lebanon was a bullet-proof vest and a steel helmet. This was standard for all foreign correspondents going north of the border. No nonsense. We looked awesome.

In the Palestinian refugee camp Anzar in Southern Lebanon I came across the phenomenon of PLO boy warriors: children only eleven to sixteen years old who were taken as soldiers by the PLO and given deadly RPG rockets to fire against Israeli forces. Nicknamed the "RPG kids," they had been in battle several times. I visited the area a few days after 221 boy fighters were released from an Israeli prison camp and handed over to the International Red Cross, which arranged for their transport home to their families.

"We let them out for humanitarian reasons," I was told by an Israeli officer, Col. Meir, who neither wanted to give his last name nor to be photographed. He told me that the Israeli authorities had decided to free all boy warriors below the age of sixteen. "But not all the prisoners know their real age," Meir said. "We release all who look like they are under sixteen, but cannot prove their age."

Many of the boys had their homes in refugee camps along the coast, and there was no problem uniting them with their families. More difficult was the situation for boys who had their homes in Syria. Their repatriation demanded a more complicated arrangement through the Red Cross. These very young guerillas, or terrorists as the Israelis termed them, are some of the most inhuman cases for which the PLO has been responsible. They were forcefully recruited to the ranks of the PLO, and many of them were sent into battle after only a short training in weaponry. Several were taken prisoner while they shot at Israeli soldiers. One of them was known to have downed an Israeli helicopter with an RPG, killing the soldiers in the aircraft.

None of the boys would admit to having fought against the Israeli troops or shot their RPGs against them. They were only schoolchildren who had accidentally ended up with the PLO and they had only peaceful intentions, they said. Many of them, however, automatically made a "V" sign with their fingers when they discovered photographers in a press group. Most of the boys looked tough, but when the Red Cross picked them up, they seemed excited and happy as if they were about to go on a school excursion. There were smiles everywhere.

They were dressed in blue jeans and white T-shirts. Their hair was closely cut or shaved off, and they had all recently showered. In their hands they each held a plastic bag with a blanket that they had received from the Red Cross. They drove away in three Red Cross trucks, which stopped every now and then and delivered a boy to his family. Some local Lebanese, however, shouted angrily "*Mehurabin*" (Arabic for "terrorists") after them.

Just before the PLO boys were sent home by the Red Cross, a prominent PLO leader visited them in the camp. He was Assaf Suleiman Abdel Khader, married to the former Jordanian queen Dina and close to the head of the PLO, Yasser Arafat. He had been the supreme commander of the Fatah forces (the largest fighting group under the PLO) in the Sidon area and had earlier headed a Fatah youth organization.

The road to Beirut with Israeli tanks

Khader, who had earlier surrendered to the Israelis, arrived at the camp blindfolded and in handcuffs. The Israelis had brought him to the camp in order for him to try to convince the boys to stop fighting the Israelis. He seemed nervous and exhausted. He said that he had surrendered to the Israelis because "the military phase of the Palestinian fight was over," as he put it. According to Khader, he surrendered only physically, but had not given up his thoughts. Asked why these small boys were trained in warfare, he said: "If you live near a river, you must teach your children to swim."

Toward the end of the war the Israelis believed that when the civilized world learned the details of the operation, Israel would be respected for fighting terror, not only on behalf of Israel, but for of others as well. "We have in fact removed the threat against other countries," a high-ranking Israeli spokesman told me. "Looking at documents we found in PLO bases in Lebanon, we saw a connection between the PLO and other terrorist organizations elsewhere in the world." This statement was in line with what Defense Minister Ariel Sharon had stated – that more than two thousand terrorists from countries all over the world had been trained in Lebanon during the past year.

The war ended on June 17 – and most of Lebanon's population felt that a long nightmare was over. Yasser Arafat had been sent into exile and the PLO in Beirut no longer existed. A young Lebanese businessman I talked to in Beirut said: "We have in fact had two nightmares. One is that the PLO forcefully took over power in major parts of our land and held many of us ransom. The other nightmare was the Israelis' heavy air attacks on PLO positions in West Beirut, causing many civilian casualties."

For Israel the price was high, not only in loss of soldiers' lives – three hundred fallen – and a cost of over $1 billion, but also in international opinion. Contrary to Israel's expectations, Israel's image in the world diminished while anti-Jewish feelings increased in many countries. Those who compared Israel's military action against the PLO to fighting sparrows with guns would probably be surprised to learn that the PLO in Lebanon had a very large force. The Israelis had thought that the PLO had eighty-nine tanks, but the actual figure was five hundred – almost half the number of tanks in the (West) German army.

According to Lieutenant Nahum, to whom I talked in Sidon, there were enough weapons, ammunition and other war material in Sidon for one hundred thousand soldiers. And in the whole area that the Israeli army held in Lebanon, enough weapons were found for at least one million men. "One may wonder where the PLO would get so many soldiers from," Nahum said, "but there are enough weapons for them."

In a basement under a seven-story building located on one of Sidon's main streets, Lieutenant Nahum showed foreign journalists an enormous ammunition depot. The room was filled with boxes containing ammunition from the Soviet Union, China and Libya for use in all kinds of weapons. Nahum said that there were thirty such depots under civilian buildings in the city. "This basement depot," Nahum said, "is an example of the tragedy in Lebanon – innocent civilians were used as PLO hostages."

I asked a woman living in the building whether she knew what the basement was hiding. "Of course," she answered. "We knew what was there. But we couldn't do anything about it. That's the way life is all over Lebanon. We were afraid of living this way, but we could not say no. While the fighting was going on, we were in a shelter deep down together with the ammunition. I am happy it is over."

While the war against the PLO in Lebanon was in its last phase, a new phenomenon appeared on Israeli roads – discharged soldiers stopping motorists and asking them and their passengers for their signatures in a petition demanding that Defense Minister Ariel Sharon step down.

In September 1982, a couple of months after the war was over, Israel's population woke up with a jolt when it learned of the massacres in the Palestinian refugee camps Sabra and Shatila near Beirut. Phalangists had entered the camps to avenge the murder of Lebanese president Bashir Gemayel. They began indiscriminately killing camp residents, and approximately seven to eight hundred Palestinians died, including women, children and babies.

The massacre reverberated throughout Israel. Then Prime Minister Menachem Begin was pressured to establish an investigative commission, headed by Supreme Court justice Yitzhak Kahan. The commission, which submitted its report in February 1983, found the Phalangists wholly responsible for the massacre, but also noted several flaws and failures on the part of some Israeli political and military leaders. While the commission determined that the Phalange were directly responsible for the mass murders, it singled out several leaders as indirectly responsible.

I was shocked to find that some of my papers in Scandinavia had chosen to change the text in my article on the verdict, indicating that Israel had been directly responsible. The letters "in" in indirectly had been omitted and had completely distorted the truth. I decided to go to Copenhagen and Oslo immediately to tell the chief editors of those papers to issue a correction. But they declined, saying that now it was an old story that one should not touch anymore. They could see that they had manipulated the facts, but shrugged their shoulders. I never expected this to happen in morally conscious Scandinavia. But it did. And I learned from several colleagues in Jerusalem, Dutchmen and Germans, that the same had occurred for them – distortion of facts to the detriment of Israel.

Painful Farewell to Sinai

In April 1982, Israel bid a painful farewell to Sinai.

The departure hurt. It was painful for eighteen-year-old Israeli soldiers to remove the many illegal settlers, who belonged to the movement "Stop the Withdrawal from Sinai." This radical movement thought that it might stop the evacuation through mass demonstrations and passive resistance.

All Israelis in the area – the illegal newcomers and the original settlers – were to leave the desert peninsula when Israel would finally withdraw on April 26, 1982. This was the price for a peace in which most Israelis did not really believe. Despite all Egyptian assurances that the peace process would continue after the Israeli withdrawal, many Israelis felt that a gradual cooling would occur in Cairo's relations with Jerusalem. Israelis on vacation in Sinai were admonished to leave the area.

Only seldom in history has a peace treaty caused people to be uprooted.

The Israeli youth were particularly skeptical. Many eighteen- and nineteen-year-old soldiers were convinced that one day, they would have to fight in the strategically important Mitla and Gidi passes – the key to Sinai. When the Israelis withdrew fifteen years after the conquest during the Six-day War in 1967, it was the third time they had retreated from the area.

The first time was in 1948. Shortly after the proclamation of the State of Israel, Egyptian forces attacked from Sinai, together with other Arab countries. Israel counter-attacked and occupied major parts of Sinai. The area was evacuated under American-British pressure.

In 1956 the story repeated itself. During the Sinai Campaign – Israel's reaction to a series of fedayeen attacks from Sinai and to a blockade of the Straits of Tiran – the Israelis again occupied the desert peninsula. They withdrew under international pressure.

During the 1967 war, Israel occupied Sinai once more. This time the Israelis refused to retreat unless their withdrawal was part of a peace treaty. The Israelis maintained that Sinai was of major strategic importance to them.

This claim was tested during the Yom Kippur War in October 1973. Thanks to the control over this vast area, Israel managed to withstand the Egyptian attack until reinforcements reached the front. If the Egyptian attack had taken place over the international border, the war would have been waged on Israeli territory.

Fanatic settlers in Yamit resisting the Israeli soldiers, who came to evacuate them

Israel had spent $17 billion during those fifteen years on development projects, of these $10 billion for defense purposes, $5 billion for developing oil sources and $2 billion for roads and civilian housing. The major part of this infrastructure, representing a value at the level of Israel's foreign debt, would be lost, if one thought only of cold figures. As part of the evacuation of Sinai, Israel gave up oil fields, air bases and military and civilian installations. The expense of moving military bases from Sinai to the Negev and relocating the civilian population to places in Israel amounted to $6 billion – and was a major reason for Israel's financial difficulties.

The biggest price, however, was surely the human one. There was deep soul-searching in Israel over the resettling of civilians. Different opinions existed as to why they had settled in the area. Many of them undoubtedly were pioneers in good faith. They believed that the government had genuinely adopted the cause, since the state sold them houses instead of renting them out. Others knew that they were building on sand, but they were ready to take the chance. The question then became whether it was fair for different Israeli governments to change their position on Sinai's status.

I decided to visit the Shangri-La–like town of Yamit, founded at the instigation of Defense Minister Moshe Dayan. A white pearl close to the Mediterranean. It had some three thousand inhabitants at the time, and they were all to leave this flourishing place by April 26. I got to the area several days before to report on facts and the mood.

It was a tragic drama. A group of twenty extremist Israelis threatened to commit suicide at rate of one every thirty minutes until only two would be left to watch over the bodies and arrange funerals. It was rumored that the Israeli army would level the town to the ground with bulldozers except for the synagogue, which would remain intact. In one of the last acts of this unfolding drama, Prime Minister Menachem Begin cabled the Israeli Editors Committee to inform them of a ban for the press, as "it surely would lead to demonstrative tragedies."

And what about Moshe Dayan, the founding father of the town? He was asked several times to go to Yamit to calm the feelings on both sides. But he never showed up.

Then a group of Israeli chief editors and representatives of journalist organizations went to Yamit to protest, knowing that they would be turned away. They were. The next day, all Israeli papers had a white space on the front page to show their protest against curbing the freedom of the press.

MFO in Sinai – What's That?

One of the many abbreviations that Sinai is full of is MFO.

Only few know that MFO stands for the Multinational Force and Observers in the Sinai and that it has been the backbone of maintaining peace between Egypt and Israel ever since it came into being in 1982. It was established jointly by Israel, Egypt and the United States to ensure that the security arrangements in the peace treaty were respected.

Twelve countries contributed troops to the force. With about seven hundred soldiers, the United States was the biggest contributor. Other countries represented in the force were Australia, Canada, Colombia, the Czech Republic, the Fiji Islands, France, Hungary, Italy, New Zealand, Norway and Uruguay. In later years, the Netherlands and the United Kingdom sent forces as well.

The Fiji contribution was very special, as this little kingdom in the Pacific with only six hundred thousand inhabitants had an army comprising four battalions, of which half served in the Middle East – one in Sinai and the other one in South Lebanon. In addition to the 340 Fiji soldiers in the Sinai, Colombia contributed the same number of men.

Italy contributed a coastal patrol, France observer airplanes, and Australia a helicopter unit. Other countries sent staff officers and observers. Norway contributed three staff officers.

But the name of Norway is all important, as a Norwegian general commands the force of about seventeen hundred troops and six hundred civilians. The Norwegian officer in charge is Major General Kjell Narve Ludvigsen; this is the fourth time a Norwegian general has served as the force commander.

When I visited the area in 1983 it was also under the command of a Norwegian officer, General Fredrik Bull-Hansen. He invited me to a helicopter tour of this vast area. We were to meet at his headquarters in the former Israeli airbase Eitam, now renamed El Gorah, some twenty miles from the Mediterranean.

I was the first foreign correspondent invited to visit MFO. Meeting me at the Rafah border crossing near Gaza was the MFO's information officer, Lieutenant Colonel David Brown, from Australia. He took me to Bull-Hansen, a tall (six feet one), authoritative man, a personality with a sense of humor. It was clear that he was well liked by his men. Bull-Hansen was quite familiar with the Middle East, having served as a captain in the UNEF force in Sinai. Among his many leading positions, he had been head of the Norwegian intelligence service.

On my helicopter tour visiting the MFO outposts in Sinai, 1983

Bull-Hansen told me that the past year had been full of interesting challenges in the operative fields. His observers had reported to him on violations of the peace agreement, on both sides. But he would not talk about these violations "because such information may be used politically by one of the parties in a way that does not further peace in this area." Bull-Hansen stressed that his force solely had the task of observing and reporting, not stopping infiltrators.

Two of the Norwegian officers in the MFO had taken part of Norway with them to the desert. They had brought their skis along and placed rollerblades under them so that they could ski on the sand.

One of the most interesting experiences during the helicopter tour was to fly over the so-called Moses Valley, where Moses, according to tradition, hit a rock with his staff and it spouted water. The valley is as an oasis in the middle of the yellow-brown desert landscape.

We landed three times at MFO observation posts. The first place was OP-14, near Yamit, manned by Fiji soldiers under command of twenty-three-year-old Corporal Sireli Lewalan. Back home in Fiji, some sixty-eight hundred miles away, he worked in a sugar factory. The next stop also had Fiji soldiers, in OP-19, further south, under command of thirty-eight-year-old Corporal Usaia Cevi. As a civilian he was a crane driver in a port. His wife and four children were in Fiji and he had committed himself to one year's service in Sinai.

The desert silence was omnipresent. But every now and then, the quiet in the area was interrupted by Bedouin Salafi's gunmen. Not long before, a group of several dozen such fighters, using some fifty vehicles, surrounded an MFO base and some sixty men stormed into the base amid heavy gunfire.

Some of the gunmen, described as Bedouin jihadists and possibly affiliated with Al Qaida, broke through the perimeter of the MFO's main North Camp. Several members of the MFO, all of them officers, were injured and evacuated to a hospital in Israel. "This is the first time anything like this has happened," an MFO spokesman said. Egyptian troops in eleven armored vehicles arrived at the base in order to help restore order.

Since then the area has been relatively tranquil, its quiet interrupted now and then by militant Bedouins.

1984 to the Present:

Struggling On

I Met a Murderer

In January 1981, Israel was gripped by one of its first political murders. A Bedouin leader and member of Knesset, Sheikh Hamad Abu Rabia, had been shot outside a hotel in Jerusalem.

The police charged three Druze men with the murder, one of whom was an officer in the Israeli army. The three were in a jeep, driving toward the Druze village of Yerka, north of Haifa, when they were caught. Two of the men could not account for what they had been doing. Police termed the arrest "a dramatic turning point."

In Knesset Abu Rabia represented the "United Arab List," affiliated with the Labor party. He had been in a bitter feud with a fellow party member, the Druze sheikh Jaber Muadi, on a rotation agreement about the Knesset seat. Muadi believed that Abu Rabia would not keep the agreement. So Muadi took action: he directed three of his sons to go to Jerusalem and kill Abu Rabia.

On a dark winter day, January 12, 1981, Muadi's three young sons – Dahesh, Seif and Har'el – drove all the way from their Druze village Yerka in northern Israel to Jerusalem in order to kill the Bedouin sheikh. They waited in ambush in a grey jeep as Abu Rabia registered at the Holyland Hotel in West Jerusalem.

Hamad Abu Rabia, head of one of the of the largest Bedouin tribes in the Negev, was known for his moderate balancing between the Israeli Labor party and militant Arab circles.

His slayers – the three Muadi brothers – were convicted of murder and sentenced to three to ten years in prison. Since the killing, the Druze feared a vendetta from the Bedouins.

Jaber Muadi quickly assumed the vacant Knesset seat after Abu Rabia's death and said he was "very sorry to return to the Knesset under such sad circumstances." He said nothing about who was responsible for the murder and indicated that Abu Rabia perhaps had been killed in a conflict over a land dispute in the Negev. He also said that the PLO had assumed responsibility for the murder. Concerning his three sons he said: "They are innocent." Father of seven sons and three daughters, Sheikh Muadi was an experienced politician and loyal toward Israel. He was seventy-nine when his sons got out of prison.

Two weeks after the murder Seif admitted that he had committed the crime, and his two brothers confessed to their complicity. Jaber Muadi himself has never been accused of anything in connection with the murder, despite the fact that he instigated it.

The Druze live mainly in a number of towns and villages in northern Israel. The village of Yerka, where the Muadi family lives, is situated a few miles east of Akko (Acre). It has some nine thousand inhabitants. In the streets one sees many religious men with their white headgear and long coats, and women wearing white headscarves.

Before the guilty verdict, Dahesh was the deputy director for the Nablus Prison, while Seif was a lieutenant in the Israeli army. The youngest son, Har'el, had completed his military service and was working as a handyman for an uncle. The three brothers were in their twenties when they followed their father's order and became murderers. How did they now feel, after all this time in prison, when the world went on while they remained behind bars? What did they think about their father who had deprived them of the best years of their lives?

These were standing questions among foreign correspondents in Jerusalem. I decided to meet the three men after they got out of prison and ask them to describe their feelings.

In this patriarchal society, I first had to contact their father. How to get to him, that was the question. I asked a Druze friend whether he could help and perhaps get me the phone number of Jaber Muadi. "No," was the answer. "Let sleeping dogs lie."

Never taking no for an answer, I contacted 144, the telephone directory service, and asked for Muadi's phone number. I got it immediately and, upon dialing, heard a man's voice on the line. I introduced myself to Jaber Muadi and asked for the number of one of his sons. Again, I got it with the greatest of ease. But Muadi also told me, "It is an old story one does not talk about anymore. It was a catastrophe."

I talked to Seif Muadi about visiting him in his Druze village in northernmost Israel and he said, "Come." So one rainy day in January 1996, I drove up the coastal road to the Druze village of Yerka. I asked my way to Seif Muadi's house and found myself in a huge hall, part of the Muadi home. I had never talked to a murderer before and wondered how the meeting would go.

Seif appeared to be a good-looking man, tall and strong, with black hair. He introduced his wife, Nadia, who did not want to be photographed for religious reasons, but consented at the request of her husband.

Seif Muadi – followed his father's wishes

"It is difficult for everybody when one wants to have a big family in a short time," Seif said. "Our last three children were born during the course of only three years after my release, and of course it was most difficult for Nadia."

"Did your two brothers also have children?" I asked him.

"Dahesh, who was in prison for three years, has five children. Har'el, the youngest, who like me was imprisoned for ten years, has two," Seif said.

"Is it true that it was you who shot Hamad Abu Rabia?"

"Yes."

"What did your brothers do?"

"They sat in the jeep."

"What did you think of on your way from Yerka to Jerusalem that day?"

"I did not think of anything. There was another mentality then."

"Can you describe the difference?"

Seif explained: "We live in a Jewish state, and this influences us strongly. For example, Nadia did not want to have her picture taken, but there are Druze women who get a driver's license and drive alone. Some years ago this was frowned upon. It was difficult for us when Abu Rabia did what he did to us – that he did not respect the agreement. We reached a point where it was difficult for us to live with this. It was not good – and what happened later was not good either. There were two bad situations. It was not right to kill and complicate things. But neither would it have been right to ignore the matter."

"Which was less bad?"

"Today I would say that it would have been better to let the situation remain as it was. But then it was awful."

"If your father had asked you today, would you have said no?"

"I would say, 'No, I do not want to kill.' If I only could have influenced my father then, we would not have come to this situation [the murder]. If one wants to sign an agreement with somebody then sign a valid agreement with the help of a lawyer. There was only a piece of paper, nothing else."

Jaber Muadi, who at one time had thought of shifting to the Likud party because he thought that Labor was not treating him appropriately, remained in Labor and even got a position from Shimon Peres. I asked

Seif how his father had been able to become a member of the Knesset after the murder.

"He was the first in line after Abu Rabia," he said. "He was not accused of murder."

"Has he not suffered as a result of this murder?"

"No, not legally, and yet he suffered. The whole family suffered."

"Your father did not tell you that you should go to Jerusalem to kill?"

"No, it was our own decision to kill. Some months before the murder, a big delegation of Druze went to Abu Rabia to talk to him, but they did not achieve anything."

"Have you forgiven your father?"

"Yes. We Druze believe one should not cry over spilt milk. I forgave him. But I am still angry."

"Was there pressure from the Druze on you and your brothers?"

"There was pressure from the Druze society on me and them and on my father. It was a stupid mistake to make such an agreement. One does not know what may happen. I am angry with the society. I forgave my father because I wanted to have peace in this matter, and I understand him."

"While you were I prison, the world changed. How do you see this change?"

"People were closer to each other then. When 'the event' occurred, the Druze supported us. During the trial in Jerusalem, many Druze came. Now people are more distant from one another. They feel they do not need each other. Compared to other communities we are one of the best, but we are not the same as before."

"What did you think when you were released after ten years?"

"That I had to go back to my family and get my life in order, work and live quietly. But there is a problem with the Bedouins. I hope they want to end the affair."

"Is there no forgiveness after all these years?"

"Still nothing. There is talk. But still nothing concrete. What happened – happened. Abu Rabia made a mistake, so did my father. We have tried to get a *sulha* [reconciliation] through the PLO. The best thing for the Bedouins and us is to forgive and finish the matter.

"What is required to make peace?"

"They must accept a delegation of respectable Druze who would go to the Bedouins and bargain about compensation. This is formal and does not concern money. The delegation will then return and report to the Druze leadership. There will be a decision and then my father, or I, will go there with white flags. Once we deserved something from them. They did not give it to us, now we owe them something. Perhaps Shimon Peres is the way to reconciliation with the Bedouins. He is a person with much clout in both groups and may bring reconciliation about. Peres is the man with that potential, but we never went to him on this. However, if we obtain a *sulha* with the Bedouins, it will symbolize peace."

To Amman via Bethlehem

I was close enough to Elias Freij, Bethlehem's mayor for many years, for him to call me his friend. Over the years we met frequently, especially around Christmas time, when he would give me the temperature of his city at yuletide.

Most of the time he was not in a Christmas mood. His city had suffered too much. He was one of the moderate Christian leaders who were on good terms with reasonable and radical Palestinians, as well as with Israelis and Jordanians.

With Freij's assistance, I got to visit the royal palace in Amman in May 1986. Freij wrote a letter in my favor to Adnan Abu Odeh, King Hussein's right-hand man. Odeh's official title was minister for the Royal Hashemite Court, but unofficially he was the man who determined Jordan's policies concerning the relationship between the PLO and Israel. Odeh was a Palestinian Arab, born in Nablus. He was a confidant of Hussein, and his political analysis of the Middle East situation was close to that of the king. It is likely that his views influenced the king's more than the other way around.

He was the eminence behind His Majesty.

The court minister's influence on Hussein was so essential that he wrote the three-hour-long speech that the monarch had delivered earlier that year, in which the king made it clear that he would no longer cooperate with the PLO to achieve a Middle East peace solution.

I went to Amman to meet Odeh, carrying Freij's letter as an introduction. It was a fairly easy trip by taxi from Jerusalem to the border on the Jordan River and again by taxi on the other side to Amman. The total distance was less than from Jerusalem to Haifa.

Amman is a pleasant, modern/ancient city, which uses traffic circles to regulate the road traffic. One of its greatest attractions is an amphitheater that dates back to Roman times.

Freij's letter to Odeh opened many doors. Soon I found myself on the wide steps leading up to the royal palace. Two guard soldiers, dressed as Circassians, were at the door and let me in after verifying that I had a meeting with Odeh. The interior of the palace was beautiful, with an Oriental touch. I met Odeh in his office in the royal palace, close to the king's quarters. I did not meet King Hussein, but Odeh told me he was nearby. At the time Odeh was fifty-three years old, a man in his prime. A handsome man too, with a black moustache.

Odeh's career spanned a long list of roles in prominent positions in the kingdom. His many different tasks showed his wide interests and unusual abilities. Odeh told me that he had a BA in literature from Damascus University and that he was contemplating leaving the king's service in order to continue his academic studies, possibly by pursuing a doctorate in political science at a university in England.

We talked mainly about the political situation in the area, focusing on the king's role in the peace process. Later I lost track of this highly gifted man, but I imagine that he continued on to other important positions.

The author with a royal guard at the entrance to the king's palace in Amman.

Jordanians Watch Israeli TV

On another trip to Amman I met the director of Jordanian TV, Muhammed Amin; the head of TV News, Ibrahim Shezadeh; and the director of the international relations department, Lina Gress. I sat across from these three Jordanian officials in Amin's office and we discussed the political situation. They knew I was coming from Jerusalem, which they found "interesting." They all agreed that the policy of the Jordanian government and the Arab League was that Israel was an enemy country.

"It is not our task to make political decisions," they said. "We believe we are powerful and objective in our relations with Israel. But we do not want to further Israel's cause – nor attack it."

Jordanian and Israeli television played an important role in the propaganda war between the two states. The Jordanian TV programs in Hebrew, English and French were popular in Israel, while the Israeli broadcasts in Hebrew and Arabic were popular in Jordan. In many sidewalk cafés and restaurants in Jordan's southernmost city, Aqaba, Israeli TV was shown throughout the afternoon as if that were the most natural thing in the world. Jordanian journalists even said that news from Israel on radio and TV was so comprehensive that Jordanian politicians would watch it in the morning to get a broad perspective on the situation in the Middle East.

"Mainly because of the language factor, the Israelis see more Jordanian TV than we see Israeli TV," news chief Shezadeh said. "Only a few Jordanians understand Hebrew, while hundreds of thousands of Israelis coming from Arab countries understand Arabic. Jordanian news broadcasts in English are a window to the world for Israelis and members of the press who do not know Hebrew."

Many of the Israelis who used to listen to these English broadcasts felt that they tended to be too anti-Israeli, to the point that they often could not recognize programs they had seen earlier on Israeli TV after

161

they got a Jordanian "slant." On the other hand, some Israelis appreciated that Jordanian TV occasionally showed scenes from Israel that unflatteringly depicted the Israeli army as an occupying force – scenes that were not shown on Israeli TV.

Many in Israel remembered when the country won the Melodi Grand Prix some years ago, but Jordanian TV covering the event skipped over all mention of the winning song. They kept it a secret from their viewers that Israel had won the song contest. About this, TV director Amin said: "Let us assume that it was an Asiatic song festival and that the PLO was represented with a song about Palestinian hopes and sufferings during the Israeli occupation – would this be shown on Israeli TV?"

Our conversation later focused on the more technical problems of Jordanian TV news in English. Regarding the Jordanian state monopoly on television Amin said: "We follow the state's directive while carrying out a kind of self-censorship. We try to maintain our professional principles. We make an effort to be critical, honest and open-minded, and we respect our viewers in an area comprising major parts of Saudi Arabia, Syria, South Lebanon to Beirut and the territories occupied by Israel."

Amin had a pragmatic perspective on Israeli TV. He watched Israeli TV every day and wanted to learn Hebrew – for professional reasons, as he put it.

Shezadeh said that the state decrees what Jordanian TV may show. He stressed: "We do not say anything good or bad about Israel," he said. "If we are in doubt, we ask the authorities for advice."

Lina Gress, who in the beginning had refrained from talking politics, also discussed a political matter by the conversation's end. "In Jordan," she said, "we have accepted Security Council Resolution no. 242. I myself come from western Jerusalem, but I am ready to refrain from every demand on our house and piece of land. This is my concession. Personally I accept Israel's right to exist."

One Million More Egyptians – Every Ten Months

Egypt's population has reached fifty-one million and now increases by one million every tenth month. How to feed all these people is one of the foremost problems of the country's leadership. Egypt imports 60 percent of its needs for food at an astronomical price, which cuts deep into its pressed economy.

Little can be done to put a brake to the population explosion. One has to find new ways to try to feed the many. "It is imperative that the primitive methods, which the Egyptian agricultural worker, the fellah, has used for centuries, be replaced by modern technology in order to increase productivity," I was told by the Egyptian minister of agriculture, Dr. Yousif Wali, in an interview in Cairo in 1987.

Dr. Yousif Wali, Egyptian minister of agriculture

He said that the cultivated area, mainly a strip along the Nile, is only some 3 to 4 percent of Egypt's 387,000 square miles. "If the Nile were properly used, the cultivated area could be doubled," he said. "The fields

163

might be radically improved if the fellah gives up traditional irrigation methods and adapts the modern drip system, developed in Israel, which takes water from a hole in the hose directly to the root of the plant."

When I talked to Wali, the agricultural production had stagnated for fifteen years, while the population increased by 2.7 percent annually. He had the responsibility for modernizing the agricultural production.

"The lack of work force is one of the reasons for the low agricultural production," Wali told me. "Many agricultural workers have moved to neighboring countries in order to work in the oil production industry, or they have moved to the cities to try to find better conditions. We encourage building greenhouses, especially in newly reclaimed areas, to cover the local needs and export vegetables and other agricultural products.

Wali articulated what only a few Egyptians dare think: that Egypt's small neighbor, Israel – with only a fraction of the water resources and work power Egypt possesses – has a highly developed agriculture and a considerable export, and that Egypt may learn a lot from this.

According to Wali, the vegetable production can be improved, and so can the utilization of export income in order to finance import and expansion of areas cultivating wheat and corn. He said that the production in fishponds must be intensified and that land reclamation should be done through cooperative enterprises or on an individual basis. He stressed that Egypt would like to cooperate with the Scandinavian countries and benefit from their professional knowledge.

He did not want to elaborate on Egypt's cooperation with Israel in agriculture. But it is known that Israeli experts in this field have been working in Egypt for several years, and that there are several joint Egyptian-Israeli research projects. Recently, Egyptian agricultural experts have been in Israel to discuss such projects with Israeli and American colleagues.

Israel has vast experience in agriculture, especially in barren areas and concerning water rationalization. It exports this know-how worldwide. Many in Egypt, however, mistrust Israel, and it is probably because of this that Wali spoke quite reservedly.

Rabin and His Stones

*Yitzhak Rabin, defense minister
1984–1990*

When the first intifada (Palestinian rebellion) began in 1988, sixty-six year-old Yitzhak Rabin was defense minister, with a promising political future. He received me for an interview in his office in Tel Aviv. At that time Israel's answer to stone-wielding Palestinian youth was a rain of small rocks and stones thrown at them from a special vehicle.

I had collected a bagful of such stones. I placed the bag on Rabin's desk and asked him, "Is this fair?" He said that it was gentler than shooting rubber bullets at the demonstrators. But he had no answer to how he could direct Israeli soldiers to break a prisoner's limbs to make him talk.

"Isn't it inhuman?" I asked. I do not remember his answer, but he was noncommittal. At that time the foreign media was full of criticism of Israel for its treatment of prisoners and for taking possession of Palestinian lands. Rabin smoked one cigarette after another. Obviously, he had a tough time being defense minister.

I asked him whether he believed gas or other chemical weapons might be used in another war, to which he answered: "If we are forced into a war, we must win it quickly and decisively, no matter what weapons the other side uses. We have to prevent a war, even wars we know we will win."

Rabin was the only senior minister in the national coalition government who held the same position he had begun with in the four-year-old

government. He did not change roles with anybody. While Prime Minister
Yitzhak Shamir was foreign minister for the first two years, and Foreign
Minister Shimon Peres was prime minister during that time, Rabin
stipulated that he wanted to be defense minister for the whole period.
This gave prestige to Rabin and peace to work in for him and his ministry.

The victor of the Six-day War in 1967, later Israel's ambassador to
the United States and later still prime minister (1974–1977), Rabin as
defense minister no doubt had one of the most demanding and responsible ministerial positions in the world. It was his job to try to overcome
the Palestinian rebellion. His workday was long and his field of work, in
addition to Israel, comprised the administered areas.

"He has a job that could take a man's life," one of his closest associates
said to me. "Many of us who are thirty years younger have problems following him." The demands of the job were visible. He looked run-down.
But no more than he had looked for the past four years. Throughout the
interview he managed to express himself in clear terms and did not react
to unpleasant questions. He looked directly and intensively at me as he
formulated his answers.

"How do you see the rocket threat during a possible new Arab-Israeli
confrontation?" I asked him.

"Israel's real security problems have been distorted," he said. "The
biggest threat against Israel's security is the constant military threat from
Arab countries that have not made peace with Israel. The arms race has
increased and taken on a new dimension. From the attacks against Tehe-
ran and Bagdad in the Iran-Iraq war we see that an important goal is to
hit the civilian population with ground-to-ground rockets. This together
with chemical warfare – for example nerve gas, which Iraq used against
Iran and against which the international community's reaction was inef-
fective – has made Israel take the military threat from Arab countries
more seriously. Syria has had these weapons for a long time, and now Iraq
has succeeded in developing the SCUD missiles which normally have a
range of 200–375 miles.

"This enables Iraq to hit goals in Israel from Iraqi territory," Rabin
went on. "The agreement between China and Saudi Arabia about deliv-
ering long-range missiles, covering a distance of twelve hundred miles

from deep within Saudi Arabia against goals in Israel, has forced us, as I said, to regard this situation more seriously."

"What is Israel's reaction to this?" was the next question.

"It is double," Rabin explained. "We have to make it clear to Arab leaders that if these weapons are used against Israel, we will reciprocate a hundred times against Arab capitals. Secondly, our people must be prepared for this threat. If these weapons are used against us in a new war, we will pay back what we have promised after a day or two."

The conversation moved to the intifada. Rabin said there was also a double goal here – to achieve quiet and make sure that the civilian administration can function efficiently and law and order are maintained in the administered areas, and at the same time to make it clear to the Arabs and the international community that the Palestinians will gain nothing from the violence.

Asked whether Soviet forces in the Middle East are a threat to Israel, Rabin answered: "Our problem with the Soviet Union concerns its politics and weapon deliveries to potential enemies of Israel. Israel has never regarded the USSR as an enemy, and we do not see the presence of a Soviet naval force in the Mediterranean as a military threat."

Rabin, born in Israel, originally had the name Rabinovitch but he shortened it. He always kept in good shape, mainly by playing tennis. Some people thought he drank too much. But the group of foreign journalists, including myself, who went with him on his tour some years ago to China, Singapore, Indonesia and Kenya did not notice any drinking problem. He was sober all the way. When we went to the Great Wall of China, Rabin was one of the first to get up. Many in his staff half his age only managed to go up with difficulty.

"How did Rabin do it – is it because he plays tennis?" somebody said.

"No," was the answer," "it is because he has played Tunis."

With Boutros-Ghali in Cairo

During my several visits to Egypt, usually as part of a group of foreign correspondents based in Jerusalem, I got a scoop when I interviewed the Egyptian diplomat Boutros Boutros-Ghali in Cairo.

It was November 1991, several weeks before he was appointed secretary general of the United Nations. I had a notion that he might win the coveted position, but he was rather unknown and I did not have any difficulty when I turned up at the foreign ministry in Cairo and asked to see him.

Boutros Boutros-Ghali, secretary general of the UN

My colleagues from Jerusalem at that time were on a tour in Cairo, visiting the Tomb of the Unknown Soldier. But I was focused on Boutros-Ghali, thinking that the experienced Egyptian politician had a much better chance than the other candidate, the Norwegian Labor politician Gro Harlem Brundtland. She later became the prime minister of Norway. "The top UN post has never been filled by a woman, and it will not happen now," I said to myself, firmly believing that I was on the right track.

Boutros-Ghali was quite popular in Israel, where in some quarters he was called Peter – a translation of his first name. He became known in international politics for the first time when he participated in President Anwar Sadat's peace overture toward Israel in 1977. He is seen as one of the main architects behind the initiative, which ultimately led to Egypt becoming the first Arab country to make peace with Israel.

For a period of fourteen years Boutros-Ghali held various ministerial posts in Egypt. In diplomatic circles he was known as a technocratic academician, who systematically tried to find negotiated solutions to international conflicts. He was educated in law with a specialty in international law. He studied at universities in Paris, Cairo and the United States, and he was an expert in North-South problems, having written several articles and books about conditions in the Third World.

As an Egyptian he declared himself both an African and an Arab and obtained support from broad circles in countries in the Third World and nonaligned states. He spoke fluent Arabic, English and French.

He was born on November 14, 1922. He married a Jewish woman, Lea Nadler, whom he met when they both studied at the Sorbonne in Paris. Boutros-Ghali – called "B.G." among friends – was a Coptic Christian, belonging to one of the world's oldest religious communities. Although he was one of Egypt's most prominent diplomats, he had never had a higher position than deputy foreign minister. When Egypt's former foreign minister, Esmat Abdel-Meguid, was appointed secretary general of the Arab League, Boutros-Ghali made it clear that he would not again tolerate being bypassed by a "junior" in the Egyptian foreign ministry.

Boutros-Ghali, however, was disappointed once more, when Egypt's former UN ambassador, Amr Moussa, was named foreign minister. As compensation Boutros-Ghali was promoted to a new position: deputy prime minister for foreign affairs. But in reality he was still deputy foreign minister. His candidacy for the UN position was by some political observers regarded as a further compensation for his lack of promotion in his homeland.

Although Boutros-Ghali was not a typical representative of black Africa, he enjoyed considerable support from African countries because of his efforts in various tasks in the Organization of African States (OAS).

Those who criticized his candidacy said that he was too old – he was sixty-nine when we met – and that his fourteen years of experience in the Egyptian foreign ministry were not enough to streamline the world organization into the demands of the twenty-first century. But

Boutros-Ghali looked younger and acted energetically for a man of his age. He had extensive international experience and – to many minds – the qualifications for the top UN job.

I was taken to his office through several corridors. He told me of his deep interest in solving the Arab-Israeli conflict and of his views on many international matters. He stressed that it was important that Africa had a representative in the position of secretary general.

"Not only is Africa the largest group in the UN, with fifty-two countries," he said, "it is also a continent that has suffered so much. My appointment would have great symbolic value for Africa and its people. When Hosni Mubarak was the president of the OAS, he said that we salute the ending of the Iron Curtain and that he believed the OAS was an important contribution to peace – but the old Iron Curtain may be replaced by a new one, between North and South. We must do what we can to contain nationalism in Africa. A secretary general from the South will show the international community the importance of Africa's problems and those of the poorer countries." Here Boutros-Ghali added, with some pride: "If you have a man with the qualifications to become UN secretary general – why not a man from Africa?"

Turning to Israeli-Palestinian relations, he said: "I believe in negotiations. They bring a new momentum and contribute to overcoming difficulties. Thus one may strengthen the moderates among Arabs and Israelis. At the same time one might curb radicals and fundamentalists who do not believe in peace and coexistence. Such elements exist among Israelis, Palestinians and Egyptians and in other Arab states. Therefore, it is important to start new peace negotiations."

I returned to Jerusalem, keeping an eye on what the UN General Assembly would decide about Boutros-Ghali. He got the appointment soon after we met. His candidacy was backed by eleven members of the sixteen in the Security Council. Some months later, Boutros-Ghali assumed the position of UN secretary general. He was the first from the African continent to fill such a top position in the UN.

Anti-terror Summit in Sharm El-Sheikh

Shortly after the assassination of Yitzhak Rabin, Israel's new prime minister Shimon Peres summoned world leaders to an international anti-terror summit meeting. The conference was meant to deal with the fight between murderous Islamic extremism and the humanistic world.

It was to be held in March 1996, in the Egyptian vacation paradise Sharm el-Sheikh on the Red Sea, with Egyptian president Hosni Mubarak and President Bill Clinton as hosts. The success of the meeting was to be measured by the extent and rank of Arab attendants. The greater the number of prominent Arab leaders that would come, the more Hamas and other organizations of terror would be isolated.

Peres was the magnet for this great endeavor. Many believed that only a man of his stature could have called for such a conference with only a few days' notice.

I was invited to cover the event and showed up among several hundred foreign correspondents. I got hold of the long list of Arab dignitaries, comprising the following: Egyptian president Hosni Mubarak, the president of the Palestinian Authority (PA) Yasser Arafat, Algeria's foreign minister Ahmed Attaf, Bahrain's crown prince Sheikh Hamad bin Isa al-Khalifa, Kuwait's foreign minister Sheikh Sabah al-Ahmad, Mauritania's prime minister Sheikh El-Afia Wil'd Mohammed Khouna, Morocco's King Hassan II, Jordan's King Hussein, Oman's special representative Thueini bin Shehab al-Said, Qatar's foreign minister Sheikh Hamad bin Khalifa Al Thani, Saudi Arabia's foreign minister Saud al-Faisal, Tunisia's foreign minister Habib Ben Yahia, the United Arab Emirates' foreign minister Rashid Abdullah al-Nuaimi and Yemen's foreign minister Abdul-Karim al-Iryani.

Some thirty Arab heads of state and ranking ministers. It was like a fairy tale out of *One Thousand and One Nights* to see all these Arab

171

monarchs, princes and other state leaders dressed in tunics with a turban or other special headgear.

The Western world was represented by the following leaders: US president Bill Clinton, Israel's prime minister Shimon Peres, UN secretary general Boutros Boutros-Ghali, Britain's prime minister John Major, France's president Jacques Chirac, Russia's president Boris Yeltsin, Canada's prime minister Jean Chretien, German chancellor Helmut Kohl, Ireland's prime minister John Bruton, Italy's prime minister Lamberto Dini, Japan's foreign minister Yukihiko Ikeda, Norway's prime minister Gro Harlem Brundtland, vice president of the European Commission Manuel Marin, Spain's prime minister José María Aznar and Turkey's president Suleyman Demirel.

The nations assembled. Left to right: Suleyman Demirel of Turkey, Hussein of Jordan, Shimon Peres of Israel, Bill Clinton of the United States, Hosni Mubarak of Egypt, Boris Yeltsin of Russia and Palestinian Yasser Arafat.

All these prominent persons were housed in luxury hotel rooms, with dreamlike gardens and fancy swimming pools.

The conference was held in a big hall in a building near one of the pools. "How to get closer to the delegates," the foreign correspondents asked themselves – and the Egyptian guardsmen standing on the other side of a tall iron gate. The foreign press demanded to get in, but were turned down and told to be patient.

I talked to one of the Egyptian soldiers and asked him how to get in. "You need a special permit," he said, but did not elaborate. "How do I get such a permit," I wondered to myself. "Perhaps in that control station up the hill?"

I went up there and talked to some men in uniforms. They asked what I wanted. "A special permit to get in," I said. They asked about my credentials and I showed them my letters of permission from the Egyptian government.

I left them and started walking downhill toward the fence when I suddenly felt that something had been put into my jacket pocket. It was the permit. I saw a man running away, toward the control station. I continued to the fence and found the soldier I had talked to.

"Is this what you want?" I said, showing him the paper I had just received.

"Exactly," he said. He let me in, to the great amazement of my colleagues.

"So far, so good," I said to myself. "What do I do next?" I found the building with the conference hall and decided to go there. I got into a large kitchen and asked for a glass of water. Then I asked: "Through which door do I enter the conference hall?" "Over there," they said.

I went through the door and there I was, in the conference room to which the foreign diplomats and other dignitaries would soon come. I was alone. I thought that I would stay on, until I was thrown out. I hung my jacket on a chair next to the one marked for Arafat. I looked around. I saw where Clinton and the American group would be seated. I photographed it all with my eyes and sensed the atmosphere.

Then I was detected. A no-nonsense guard bodily removed me from the hall. But I had registered everything and had enough material to write a colorful story, even before the conference began.

After I was thrown out, I rearranged my cameras and joined the line of photographers waiting to get in and take pictures of this historic event. The world photographers looked at my modest equipment and wondered who I was. But I could write a detailed, descriptive story, different from what others would do.

The theme of the conference was "the summit of the peacemakers," who should join forces to combat international terror and actively work for keeping the Middle East peace process on track. The intention of the meeting was to try to show the victory of good over evil. It was a great support for the Israeli people who at the time were depressed over the many Israelis killed in meaningless attacks.

Not least it was a support of Prime Minister Shimon Peres, who together with Clinton and Mubarak had taken the initiative for the conference.

The Russians Are Coming

The Russian Jews started coming to Israel in great numbers in the early 1990s, after Moscow agreed to liberalize its policy toward the Jews in return for improved American trade and credit arrangements, and now more than a million Russian Jews live in Israel. In the beginning, Russian authorities told would-be immigrants that they had to repay for their education at Russian universities first, but this Russian policy was soon abandoned.

Immigrants arriving in Israel

The Russian Jews constitute some 15 percent of Israel's population of 8 million. Translating this percentage to the American population of 293 million, it would mean an increase of some forty million new Americans over a ten-year period. An overwhelming, almost incomprehensible figure. Yet, this was what happened in Israel. The Jewish state took in wave after wave of Soviet Jews, mainly from Ukraine and Russia. This massive immigration, which many thought would be an unbearable strain on a country as small as Israel, has in reality become a great boon to its economy.

The Russians contributed to bringing Israel away from the Orientalization that was beginning to take hold in the country. Long ago, when the Sephardi (Oriental) part of Israel's population started to make inroads among the ruling Ashkenazi (European) inhabitants, Israel began looking like a completely different country from the one the world got to know when the state was established in 1948.

At that time there was the stereotypical conception of Israel as a Western country, even though it was situated in the Middle East. It was understood that Israel was a modern, developed and democratic country with almost European norms of liberalism, humanism and rationalism. However, Israel was already well on its way to becoming a "Levantine" country, for good and for bad (the Levant is an old term for countries in the eastern part of the Mediterranean). The change toward Orientalization could perhaps best be seen in the 120-seat Knesset, whose members of Oriental background kept increasing, from twenty-one in 1977 to thirty-two in 1984. The mass immigration from Russia completely changed this almost overnight and renewed Israel's European character – a revolution from within.

While many thought that little Israel would sink under the burden of the massive Russian-Jewish immigration, it managed in a few years to integrate the million newcomers to the benefit of all. Many of the Russian immigrants are academicians. Although the Russians come from eastern Europe and Asia, a major part of them are Western in mind.

The first Russian Jews came to then Palestine in the 1880s, and many more arrived over the years. Formerly, it was not unusual that close to 10 percent of the immigrants to Israel, during their first few years, would emigrate because they could not adapt to life in Israel. This phenomenon hardly exists with the last wave of immigrants. Only 1 to 2 percent could not manage the conditions in Israel and left.

All newcomers to Israel go through the same trauma of getting adjusted to the climate and the Israeli society, learning a new language, finding work – either in their own profession or after being retrained – and finding accommodation. But the longer new immigrants are in Israel, the more their economic situation improves. In a study by the

Geocartographic Institute covering a six-year period, it was reported that the standard of living for immigrants from the former Soviet Union had soared faster than in the general Israeli population.

According to the Jewish Agency, the main reasons for immigration from the former USSR were evenly split between concern over the future of their children, family reunion and Zionist aspirations. Israel has welcomed the Russian immigration for ideological reasons. Despite problems, most of the immigrants have succeeded in creating good lives for themselves in Israel. Many of them feel it is a great relief to live as Jews without anybody shouting after them in the street or at work.

In 1987, two new Jewish immigrants told me the story of their immigration and how they had managed economically. They were a young married couple, both of them in their early twenties, and both with degrees in economics.

The wife's name was Julia; she was originally from Moscow. The husband was named Tevikes Raudanskis, from Kovno in Lithuania. Their families had lived in those cities for generations, until they and their parents decided to settle in Israel. They both began studying for a degree in economics at the Technion Institute of Technology in Haifa, which is where they met.

Julia got a BA in economics and had started working in a bank, while Tevikes had a BS in economics, but – when we met – had not found the right position. They lived in a small three-room rented apartment in Haifa; they were hoping to save enough money to buy their own place in a few years.

The tsunami of Russian-Jewish immigrants had a social lopsidedness, which was widely mentioned in Israeli media when the immigration peaked. There was prostitution among some of the newly arrived Russian women, who supplemented the meager family income through woman's oldest profession. Shoplifting from supermarkets trebled some years ago, mainly due to the new immigrants. And soup kitchens were established for immigrants who did not see any other way than this one in order not to go to bed hungry. Those days are over, but they were an eyesore in the beginning of the immigration wave.

Many of the new immigrants had to change their professions in order to have a decent income. A large number of them were in the field of music, and it was said that there were enough good Russian-Jewish musicians to have a symphony orchestra in even small towns. Israeli schoolchildren benefited, as they were taught music by professional Russian immigrant musicians who could not find any other employment.

The immigration medal, however, had a dark other side. Some twenty years ago, more than one hundred thousand of the immigrants were single women, and a high percentage of them were listed as divorced or widowed, caring for one or more children.

Many of them knew that they were Jews only because it was written in their official papers and because they were discriminated against in the Former Soviet Union. Upon their arrival in Israel, a large number of them hardly felt an ethnic identification with Jews – seventy years of communism had almost erased their Jewish identity.

I talked to several of these women, including Lena, aged forty-four from St. Petersburg, who lived in a three-room rented apartment in Jerusalem with her fifteen-year-old daughter Katja and her parents. Lena worked as a guide at the Israel Museum. When we met she was deeply depressed because she did not know how she would be able to use her immigrant's rights to obtain a loan for buying an apartment. A small apartment would cost 1 million NIS (about $250,000), and if she could not get the state's subsidy within one year and close on a deal, she would forfeit those immigrations rights. No wonder she was depressed.

The most well-known among Russian Jews who have come to Israel is undoubtedly Anatoli Sharansky, whose mother spoke to me from Moscow before he made his journey to freedom.

The Russian-Jewish immigration to Israel is regarded as a genuine success story, not least because of the resilience of these newcomers.

Gaza: The Time Bomb

The Gaza Strip faces an enormous population increase – three million in twenty-five years.

During the first Palestinian uprising (intifada) against the Israeli occupation, the leadership of the PLO endorsed a measure that a high birthrate was a national duty. Palestinian women were urged to use their womb as a weapon and to produce a maximum number of warriors for the Palestinian cause, in order to achieve a population of five million, almost equal to that of the Israelis.

The masses complied with the request. But what began as a political success almost became a national disaster for the Palestinians. Their birthrate is so high – seven children per family in Gaza on average – that the leader of the Palestinian Statistics Department, Hassan Abu Libveh, said that "we are now faced with a demographic time bomb."

Gaza squalor

The Palestinian birthrate of 3.5 to 4.5 percent per year is probably the world's highest. At the same time the infant mortality rate has fallen considerably from 140 per thousand in the 1970s, to 50 ten years ago and to 28 in our day. According to Abu Libveh, the Palestinian population in Gaza – one million – will be doubled in the next seventeen years, and tripled eleven years later. It is almost impossible to imagine that three million people will be able to live in such a small region.

Gaza's leadership is facing an enormous challenge. However, much is going on in Gaza these days, in different areas. Many large private homes are being constructed, often in the vicinity of low-rise slum dwellings.

In order to understand how Gaza will try to accommodate three million people, I visited the area and met with representatives of the UN and leading Palestinians in the education, healthcare and social sectors. The UN representative in charge of the world organization's aid to refugees, UNRWA (United Nations Relief and Works Agency), was the Danish professor Peter Hansen. Among the Danes working in the UN system, Peter Hansen occupied the highest position. Hansen was born in Aalborg. In 1966–67 he taught political science at Aarhus University and during the period 1976–78 he was employed as professor in the department of political science at Odense University. He came to the UN in New York as assistant secretary general for planning and program budgeting. Peter Hansen said with a smile that he had set a "world record" as he had been on leave of absence from his work in Denmark for more than twenty years.

In 1996 the then UN Secretary General Boutros Boutros-Ghali asked Hansen to become the secretary general for UNRWA. With headquarters in Gaza and Amman, UNRWA supports 3.5 million Palestinian refugees in Jordan, Lebanon, Syria, the West Bank and the Gaza Strip in the areas of education, healthcare and social welfare.

Asked what an ideal solution in the area would look like, Hansen replied: "Apart from the fact that an ideal solution should be in accordance with the different UN resolutions for the area, it is impossible right now to see whether the main parties in the peace process have anything that resembles a common viewpoint. The Palestinians insist on UN resolution no. 194 [concerning the Palestinian refugees' right of return], while Israeli negotiators maintain that a right of return is out of the question.

Probably the only way to solve the problems in this area," Hansen said, "is through negotiations with the parties."

The conversation moved to speculation over whether monetary aid from abroad has landed in the wrong pockets as a result of corruption. Peter Hansen strongly rejected that this could be the case.

"Naturally no organization can say 'We are not corrupt,'" he said. "We ourselves have had some instances of corruption, such as when we discovered that some of our drivers had smuggled cigarettes between Syria and Jordan. They were fired immediately. We have also exposed a colleague who falsified a data processing report regarding hospital bills, which was discovered by our own internal audit. The accusations of corruption were raised by a former coworker, who was not rehired. Scotland Yard and other police forces were asked to investigate the affair. The accusations led nowhere."

Commenting on the forecast of three million inhabitants in Gaza in twenty-five years' time, Peter Hansen said: "There will be a population explosion if the present growth curves are automatically increased. Gaza already has the biggest population growth in the world, 5 to 6 percent annually, which is caused by, among other things, a high birthrate and a significant immigration of Palestinians from different countries following the Oslo Accords."

Asked what could be done to improve the situation, the UNRWA secretary general said that in the first place, social and economic improvement must be attained in order to slow down the population growth. "It has been seen elsewhere in the world that the birthrate declines with an improvement in the economy," said Peter Hansen. "Provided there will be peace and prosperity in the area, the demographic development will stabilize. Spacing of births is now mentioned in connection with family planning, so that there will be longer intervals between the children. The very short periods between births can be found among the very religious here – just like in Israel."

According to Peter Hansen the worst scenario would be that the entire Gaza Strip would be as overpopulated as the Shatila refugee camp, where sixty-five thousand people are stowed together in an area of 0.2 square miles.

I also met with the person in charge of UNRWA's education program in Gaza, Dr. Ahmed Mousa and his female assistant Mahasen Muhasen. Dr. Mousa said that basically all children under the age of fifteen attend compulsory elementary school, that 30 percent continue on to high school and that 10 to 15 percent go on to one of Gaza's two universities with a total of thirty-nine thousand students, or to the teachers' college, which comprises five thousand students. He says that the number of students has risen substantially, because twelve thousand students returned from other countries following the Oslo Accords.

"We are faced with a serious dilemma," said Dr. Mousa. "The increase in the number of students is considerable, 6 to 9 percent per year, the highest in the world."

"Can Gaza cope with this situation?"

"We have no material resources in Gaza," Dr. Mousa said. "Three thousand people live here in an area of 0.3 square miles, while there are only 144 people to 0.3 square miles in the West Bank, where large undeveloped areas can be put to use."

According to Mousa, one-third of Gaza's population – some 350,000 – attend school and that children under the age of fifteen constitute half of the area's population.

When asked how modern thinking can be reconciled with the strong, religious rules of Islam, Dr. Mousa replied: "The answer is education, not least in family planning, so that people can live under decent conditions. But if they do not see an alleviation of their misery, they will turn to religion. We must create work and education programs so that we can keep up with the twenty-first century and improve the quality of life. We should have fewer children. Unfortunately the economic situation has worsened, but this is widely accepted as a transitional phenomenon. Should the economic conditions not improve soon, the situation will become very serious."

Mahasen Muhasen told that twenty-five years ago the women in Gaza were ignorant of such issues as healthcare, family planning and child vaccinations, but today they are better informed. The assistant manager of UNRWA's aid and social programs in Gaza, Kamal Abu Qamar, said that some of the biggest problems are a result of whole families being crowded together in one room in small refugee dwellings. "The economic and housing problems are acute," he said. "The divorce rate is 16 percent, and there is serious unemployment. Moreover, there is violence within the families, parents against children, husbands against wives."

The ancient city of Gaza was located on one of the main thoroughfares of ancient times, the Roman Via Maris, which ran between Egypt and other countries in the Middle East; the precise location of ancient Gaza City is unknown today. In chapter 16 of the book of Judges in the Old Testament, the story is told of Delilah who captured her fiancé, Samson the giant, and turned him over to Gaza's Philistines in exchange for eleven hundred silver shekels. When he died, Samson avenged himself on the Philistines. Other large Philistine cities were Ashdod, Ashkelon, Ekron and Gat. Throughout history, Gaza has been governed by the Egyptians, the Philistines, the Hebrews, the Assyrian Empire, the Babylonians, the Persians, the Greeks, the Hasmoneans, the Romans, the Byzantine Empire, the Arabs, the Crusaders, the Egyptian Mamluks, the Ottoman Empire (during which time the French, under Napoleon, briefly conquered Gaza), the British, the Egyptians and the Israelis.

From 1917 to 1948 the Gaza Strip was a British mandatory area, established by the League of Nations. After the establishment of Israel in 1948 and the armistice agreements with Arab countries in 1949 the area came under Egyptian administration (except for six months of Israeli occupation in connection with the Sinai Campaign in 1956). Gaza's inhabitants, however, never obtained Egyptian citizenship and remained stateless.

As part of the Six-day War in 1967, the area again came under Israeli control. Since then, part of the area's workforce has found employment in Israel.

The Gaza Strip is a twenty-six-mile long and four-to-six-mile wide rectangular area of approximately 140 square miles, with a population of about one million, which is expected to grow to three million by the year 2030.

In Arabic Gaza is called "Qita' Ghazzah" and in Hebrew "Retzuat Azza." The largest city in the area is Gaza city with 400,000 inhabitants. Other major cities are Khan Younis, a central city with a population of

200,000, and Rafah in the south with 150,000 people. Gaza's inhabitants mainly make a living by cultivating citrus fruit and olives, cattle grazing and a little fishing. There is a small building industry.

Only few know that Jewish history in Gaza goes 3700 years back. Some know the earlier mentioned biblical story of Samson, who was blinded by the Philistines and had his revenge in Gaza. But only a small number know that for thousands of years Jews had a flourishing community in Gaza.

The Gaza Strip might have been known as the place to which Moses went with tens of thousands of Israelites after the exodus from Egypt. After leaving Egypt, the shortest route to the Promised Land would have been through the Gaza Strip. However, the Old Testament reveals that the Jewish people were instead led through the desert, out of concern that a confrontation with the Philistines would prove overwhelming for the newly freed Israelites (Ex. 13:17–18).

I have been to Gaza many times to report from there. It is always with apprehension I cross into the area where it is important to have a Palestinian connection to guide one around and arrange meetings. Gaza – the word itself gives the notion of violence, gruesome conditions, poverty, overpopulation and human degradation.

How to change this nobody knows.

The Worried Copts

The Coptic Christians in Egypt are worried.

Once a majority in Egypt, they now make up about 10 percent of the country's eighty-six million people. They are the largest Christian community in the Middle East. Their history dates back nineteen centuries, and the language used in their liturgy can be traced to the speech of Egypt's pharaohs.

They are worried because radical Islamists have made deep inroads into the Egyptian society, and subsequently many Copts feel the breathing down their backs. This has resulted in a steady increase in Coptic immigration to the United States and elsewhere.

Michael Saad, chairman of the Council for Coptic Studies at Claremont Graduate University in California, says: "The numbers of emigrants have greatly increased over the past eighteen months, since the so-called Arab Spring in December 2010. There are very few left in every church."

In one of my visits to Cairo I met a young Copt who agreed to talk about their situation, provided he could speak anonymously. He did not know the actual number of Copts in Egypt, but thought that 10 percent of the population was exaggerated.

This Copt, a twenty-six-year-old surgeon at the hospital in Cairo, said that the polarization between Egypt's Muslims and Copts often leads to violence. Muslim fundamentalists have tried to burn down two Coptic churches, in revenge for the Copts' arson of a mosque.

"The attack on the mosque was just a rumor, and police believes that the fire was due to a short circuit," the young doctor said. "In another city Muslim demonstrators tried to burn down a Coptic church, following rumors that Copts had tried to draw a cross on veiled Muslim women by use of a spray bottle."

The doctor said that both Muslims and Copts are God fearing, but that religions may be misused. "We Copts fear Muslim fundamentalism, which wants to take over power. If this happens, time will be set back a hundred years."

A middle-aged Egyptian I talked to said that the basic difference between the two population groups is that while the Christians believe they follow God's words, the Muslims follow – God. Thereby they are closer to him. "The Muslim fundamentalists are gaining in Egypt, as well as in the Arab world," this man said. "Their goal is to achieve a state order that follows a strict interpretation of Islamic law, the shariah, prohibiting pork and alcohol."

He told me of an episode at the medical faculty in one of Cairo's universities. The dean of the faculty banned women students to come veiled to the lectures, because – the dean said – it prevents contact between physician and patient. "It developed into a confrontation. To begin with the dean's views prevailed, but then he was attacked by long-bearded students, who wanted to punish him."

The attraction to fundamentalism is especially common among the lowest in society. They see Egypt's hard-pressed economic situation as completely hopeless and want to try another way.

Peres – Old and Wise

At the age of ninety, Shimon Peres stepped down from Israel's presidency. He served as head of state for seven years, ending in 2014. He has set an example for people all over the world of what one may still achieve in old age.

Shimon Peres, ninety years old and still going strong

Peres has turned into a wise man, whom world leaders listen to, not least for his visionary ideas for a better Middle East. For Israel he is one of the last of the state's founding fathers, David Ben-Gurion's disciples, the man who brought atomic power within Israel's reach, the architect behind building the country's air force to a formidable power and the clever politician who has now finally come out on top. For many years the Labor politician Peres was the number two man in Israeli politics, but at the 2007 election for presidency he came in number one.

I have met him countless times – in his office for an interview, at cocktail parties, in the Knesset. He is a polite man, known for being more fit than many who are much younger.

But there is another side of Peres as well. He is known also as a schemer, a master of double talk and political tricks. I remember him in that role when he pretended not to know that the foreign press would be present at a meeting he had with visiting academicians from abroad. He coyly said that now he could not speak freely because of the presence of foreign journalists. But he knew full well that they would be there.

He also caused lifted eyebrows when he, as a government minister, did not prevent settlers from building the illegal Sebastia outpost on the West Bank, and through his inaction encouraged the settlers to spread over still larger areas. Many also remember his eternal rivalry with Yitzhak Rabin for the top leadership position.

All of this is history. During the last thirty years Peres has turned into a well-polished world politician, perhaps Israel's only statesman in the full sense of the word. Peres is one of the very few who can summon a gathering of world leaders. He did so at Sharm el-Sheikh in Egypt, when he called world leaders for an anti-terror conference shortly after the murder of Rabin. And he did it again when he turned ninety in June 2013.

Many Israelis criticized him for not being more modest and for putting himself in the spotlight too much. But there were also people who came to his defense. Columnist Rachel Kleimen wrote: "Peres is entitled to celebrate his birthday a whole month, if he wants it. He has lived several lives – at least professionally, and he needs more than one day to celebrate."

World stars and other celebrities streamed to Jerusalem last June to celebrate with Peres during several days of festivities. Among the well-wishers were President Bill Clinton, Barbra Streisand, Robert De Niro, Sharon Stone, England's former prime minister Tony Blair (now a special envoy to the Middle East peace process), Russia's Mikhail Gorbachev, Rwanda's president Paul Kagame and Prince Albert of Monaco. A total of twenty Emmy, Grammy, Nobel and Oscar winners came to celebrate Peres.

Peres told me that he works out early every morning, which may account for his fitness. He is a workaholic, busy from morning to late evening. He goes frequently on state visits abroad and looks much younger when he marches past an honorary guard.

He is the Israeli who is most recognized and appreciated abroad.

The Prince and I

It's been over nine hundred years between visits of Scandinavian royals to Jerusalem.

At the end of October 2013, Danish crown prince Frederik visited Israel to attend a gala concert at the Jerusalem Theater. The event marked the seventieth anniversary of the Danish people's rescue of Denmark's seven thousand Jews to Sweden in October 1943 during the German occupation of Denmark.

The rescue operation – the only light in the darkness of Nazi-occupied Europe – was almost completely successful as about 90 percent of Danish Jewry was saved. The crown prince's visit was yet another milestone in Denmark's relationship with the Jewish people. His visit was of course not political, but it was significant in that it represented yet another outstretched Danish hand to the Jews and perhaps also a special recognition of Israel in troubled times.

It was a historic visit. Not for 906 years had a Nordic king visited Israel. The last one was that of Norwegian king Sigurd Jorsalfar (Norwegian for "Jerusalem traveler"), who was here on a pilgrimage toward the end of his reign (1103–1140) and who was the leader of a Norwegian crusade. Another Scandinavian king set out for Jerusalem, but never quite made it. He was Danish king Erik Ejegod ("Erik the Ever Good"), who wanted to come on a pilgrimage but died in Cyprus in 1120.

Crown Prince Frederik, aged forty-five, is highly educated in political science and military and diplomatic matters. Perhaps above all, he is an avid sportsman, in marathon running, sailing, swimming, diving, parachuting and tennis. He is a frogman in the navy, where he goes by the nickname "Pingo" – and he won the hearts of most Danes when some years ago he set out on a grueling month-long sledge-dog patrol in the Greenland darkness.

I met Denmark's future king at a reception following the gala concert. We got into a deep conversation about his recent visit to the

Yad Vashem Holocaust institution commemorating the six million Jews killed by the Nazis. He shared his impression upon seeing there the small Danish boat used in the rescue operation for the Danish Jews, and I told him how I had brought the rescue vessel to Israel.

"And what are you doing now?" the crown prince inquired.

"When the royal visit is over, I shall write my journalistic memoirs," I responded.

"I would like to have an early copy," Crown Prince Frederik said.

www.ingramcontent.com/pod-product-compliance
Lightning Source LLC
LaVergne TN
LVHW061326060426
835511LV00012B/1889